choices
for the high school graduate
Fourth Edition

A Survival Guide for the Information Age

Bryna J. Fireside

Checkmark Books®

An imprint of Facts On File, Inc.

Choices for the High School Graduate, Fourth Edition

Copyright © 2005 by Bryna J. Fireside

Ferguson
An imprint of Facts On File, Inc.
132 West 31st Street
New York NY 10001

Library of Congress Cataloging-in-Publication Data

Fireside, Bryna J.
    Choices for the high school graduate / Bryna J. Fireside.—4th ed.
    p. cm.
    Includes bibliographical references and index.
    ISBN 0-8160-5594-7(alk. paper)
    1. Student aspirations—Handbooks, manuals, etc. 2. Student aspirations—United States—Handbooks, manuals, etc. 3. Vocational guidance—United States—Handbooks, manuals, etc. 4. College student orientation—United States—Handbooks, manuals, etc.
5. Career development—United States—Handbooks, manuals, etc. I. Title.
    LB1027.8F58 2004
    373.18'0973—dc22   2004040656

Ferguson books are available at special discounts when purchased in bulk quantities for businesses, associations, institutions, or sales promotions. Please call our Special Sales Department in New York at (212) 967-8800 or (800) 322-8755.

You can find Ferguson on the World Wide Web at http://www.fergpubco.com

Text design by Mary Susan Ryan-Flynn
Cover design by Cathy Rincon

Printed in the United States of America

MP JT 10 9 8 7 6 5 4 3 2 1

This book is printed on acid-free paper.

For Harvey Fireside, with whom I
continue to share so many great adventures.

TABLE OF CONTENTS

ACKNOWLEDGMENTS

It was my good fortune to interview dozens of young people for this book. Thank you one and all for taking the time to share your experiences with me. I only wish that I could have used all the stories I collected, but alas, that just wasn't possible. I deeply appreciate the time given to me by college administrators and by the people who direct many of the organizations mentioned in this book. A special thanks to Peter Francese, founder of *American Demographics Magazine,* for his concise and insightful comments on what kinds of careers are going to be in demand for you who are soon to graduate high school and are considering your options. Thanks, too, to Dr. Carl Haynes, president of Tompkins-Cortland Community College, for sharing some of the exciting new developments that community colleges teach in the Information Age.

And finally, I thank my own three children, who managed to give me numerous heart-stopping moments as they tore through their "terrible teens." They each made their way into adulthood with a surprising amount of smarts, good sense, and social conscience. Were it not for their daring to break the rules of traditional lockstep education, I would not have dared to write this book.

"In this rapidly changing environment, if you're not confused, you're not thinking clearly."
—Burt Nanus, author of *The Leader's Edge: The Seven Ways to Leadership in a Turbulent World*

SEVERAL YEARS AGO I INTERVIEWED DOZENS OF YOUNG PEOPLE, COLLEGE ADMINISTRATORS, PARENTS, AND TEACHERS FOR A BOOK I CALLED *CHOICES: A STUDENT SURVIVAL GUIDE FOR THE 1990S*. I hoped that by letting young adults talk about their quest, they would help others see that it isn't always necessary or right to accept someone else's notion of how to grow up. There are times when taking that quirky bend in the road is exactly right.

Well, here we are with both feet in the 21st century. In some ways the world is changing at a dizzying pace. It is almost as if the excitement of a new century demands all kinds of new ways to speak, travel, work, and play. Already we study, communicate, learn, and work in ways that weren't possible just six or seven years ago—or even yesterday. People are using terms such as "the wireless workplace," "slogging," and "file sharing." Words such as "text messaging" and "spam" roll off the tongues of seven-year-olds who have to explain them to their parents. These were not part of our ordinary vocabulary a couple of years ago. The truth is that computers have revolutionized the way teachers teach and students study and learn. The answer to just how much computers have changed the way education is being "delivered" (yes, there are people who actually believe education is something to deliver—like pizza!) is still being assessed. Indeed, not all the questions have been asked, even though colleges and universities are rushing to adapt their campuses to the new technologies needed for distance learning. Professors are urged to develop new courses to be offered on the Web, or to teach a course at one college while students from another sit in front of a TV screen and interact with the professor and other students in the actual classroom. It may take years before students and professors can honestly evaluate a "virtual college education" as compared to a traditional one where professors and students are on a real college campus in a real classroom, discussing course material face-to-face. (However, just how much our world depends upon the new technology becomes abundantly clear each time we have a disastrous power failure, such as the one that brought life in the Northeast and parts of Canada to a halt on August 14, 2003.)

Just a few years ago, most students who applied to colleges did so by sending for college catalogs (now known as "viewbooks"—see, we even have a totally new vocabulary) and applying to anywhere from one to five or six colleges and universities, one by one. Today you can quickly check out twenty or thirty colleges as you sit in your room with your computer, or if you don't have one, using the computer in your high school or public library. Professor Diane Gayeski of the Park School of Communications at Ithaca College (Ithaca, New York) says, "A student who just relies on the catalog through the mail will be missing out and will only be getting the older, typical experience. Computer technology gives a more in-depth and credible picture of who the alumni are and who the professors are and what they have published."

And Linda Miller, Associate Dean of Admissions at the University of Virginia at Charlottesville, looks forward to the day when "all applications can be done through computers. It will be a lot less expensive, because mailing is a huge problem and is very expensive. We get 17,000 applicants, [although] we mail out 40,000-plus applications. To have our catalog and course offerings on the Web is a huge savings, not only for the university, but also for the applicant. A prospective student can ask questions and get answers far more easily on the Web than if they wrote letters. Kids now have instant access to the colleges."

But even without access to computers, you don't have to be afraid that the traditional method of applying to college will become obsolete. "It is important," says Miller, "that we have all methods of applying available."

Because new technology seems to be forcing us to make changes in all areas of our lives, I think it's time for another look at what kinds of choices are out there for you and what kinds of skills you will need to succeed in this new Information Age. Actually, it's still the same old world it was before—only now it's enhanced by a lot of great gadgets that even the most bumbling among us will eventually be called upon to use.

Your generation will spend its entire adult life in the twenty-first century. Older folks, who remember being thrilled with electric typewriters, are all thumbs now that they have to grapple with this new technology and its tongue-twisting vocabulary. (I even remember the excitement over ballpoint pens versus ink pens. No, I never did write with a quill, but I do have a great artist friend who loves working with special inks and a sharpened turkey feather. He turns out exquisite works of art that simply can't be duplicated by a computer, although the computer can produce some very attractive art, too.)

What's exciting for you is that you already possess some of the greatest assets for success in the twenty-first century:

1. You are young and enthusiastic.
2. You have the ability to absorb all this new technology easily because you don't have to unlearn the old ways of communicating and working.
3. You are full of new and fresh ideas, and you understand how to make this new technology work for you. You can run spell check to catch your spelling errors, use a talking

or Braille computer if you are blind, and employ a computer notepad to turn your handwritten scribbles into typed notes from which to study—and so much more.

Today, business leaders and college presidents talk about the next stage of computers that will make communicating through the Internet or interactive television as easy and as inexpensive as talking on the phone or turning on the radio. We're not quite there yet, but we are rapidly moving in that direction. Although we don't have to worry that the traditional college campuses will become obsolete, what we will see is that the world has become a much smaller place thanks to the rapid expansion of technology. Unfortunately, since 9/11, the world has also become a more dangerous and somewhat unpredictable place. But there are myriad opportunities out there.

HUMAN BEINGS HAVEN'T CHANGED

No matter how fast technology changes the way we work and learn, we mere human beings don't change much at all. We still start out as infants, grow into little kids, make it to high school— and we still have to figure out what to do with our lives. In the nineteenth century, people didn't have a choice about the kind of work they did. A man did what his father did, and if you were a woman, you married someone your father chose for you and lived a life much the same as your mother's. The Industrial Revolution in the twentieth century moved us into the cities, where people began to exercise more choices.

ENDLESS CHOICES

Here in the twenty-first century the concept of work is changing again. Men and women in the Information Age can expect to change jobs every few years. Many of you already have seen one or both parents change jobs several times—all too often because they were laid off from a job at a company they believed would employ them until retirement.

You will probably change your job as many as six or seven times, and you may also totally change careers. You will find work and leisure activities that use a whole range of your talents. And instead of feeling as if your formal education is over once you graduate from college or other postsecondary training, you will need to think of yourself as a lifelong learner—one who continually looks for opportunities to update skills and acquire new information. Becoming an educated and employable person takes on a whole new meaning in the Information Age.

No matter how much the world changes, you are concerned right now with finding answers to the same important questions teenagers have been asking since the beginning of time:

Who am I?
Why am I here on this planet?
What am I supposed to do with my life?
Will I find someone to love, and will he/she love me back?
Am I going to be able to find work that means something more than just a paycheck?
Can I support myself?
Am I smart enough, good looking enough, tall/short enough?
Will I find friends?
What are my choices?
Do I have to follow in someone else's footsteps?
Do I really have to grow up?

These are the really important questions, and each of us must find the answers in our own way and in our own time. The people you will meet in this book grappled with these issues, too. Some, like Doug Leonard, reached a point where school seemed boring and useless. Doug wanted to quit and get a job. He knew he would go to college at some point, but, he said, "I needed to find out who I was."

Others were more like Lorin Dytel, who had gotten everything she could out of high school by the time she finished her sophomore year. She was ready for college just after her sixteenth birthday. To win support for her desire to go to college early, Lorin had to battle not her parents, but her high school teachers and guidance counselors.

Nate Kipp, on the other hand, dutifully went off to college after high school without a clue as to what he wanted to do. After a painful year in which he found out he wasn't ready for college, he decided to take time out. Nate heard about AmeriCorps and took two years to do some serious community service with Habitat for Humanity.

Brian Millspaugh determined that he was a "hands-on" sort of learner. In his junior year of high school he signed up for the electricians' course at his local BOCES (Board of Cooperative Educational Services). In the mornings, he took regular classes at his Trumansburg, New York, high school, and in the afternoon, he learned how to become an electrician. A year after he graduated from high school, he went to the electrical workers' union and took the qualifying exam to become an apprentice. He gets paid during his four-year apprenticeship leading to a journeyman's license and a career as a commercial electrician.

Dan Elsberg honed his Spanish language skills by volunteering for two summers with Amigos de las Americas, a group that promotes good health in South American countries by sending in teams of young people to inoculate children against polio, measles, and other devastating childhood diseases. He did this while he was still in high school—and came to understand, appreciate, and value people from different cultures.

Each of these students, as well as others you will meet in this book, felt like square pegs in round holes for a while. But instead of trying to fit in where they didn't belong or didn't want to be, these students struck out on their own. All have taken risks, done the unexpected . . . and survived. In fact, most have become solid citizens whom their parents are proud of. Not surprisingly, others needed to take more time to figure out their lives and are still searching. The things they did helped them all develop the confidence to tackle new situations and fearlessly break away from the pack. In this book, you will meet kids who learned how to think through their options and make decisions. They learned how to argue constructively with their parents and guidance counselors—even their friends. They learned how to relate to and work with people who were vastly different from themselves. And each learned how to manage his or her time. Curiously enough, they developed the skills the experts tell us successful people will need in the unpredictable future.

Not everything they tried was an unqualified success. Sometimes a coveted job, internship, or community service project turned out to be awful. Michael Urgo thought he was going to land a great job in a ski town in British Columbia, only to find out the job didn't exist—and as a U.S. citizen, he wasn't able to get a work visa. More than one person went to college as an early admission student, only to feel overwhelmed by the challenge and doubtful about the choice. More often than not, though, the fear of failure and the possibility of someone saying "I knew it wouldn't work" were enough to keep the person going until things improved.

Even seemingly unhappy experiences had their own peculiar set of rewards. The old saying "If life hands you lemons, make lemonade" applied in some tough situations. If there is a common thread that runs through all of the interviews, it is that by maintaining a tremendous spirit of adventure and moving out in new directions, kids, many just like you, felt they were in control of their lives. Even adversity has its rewards.

I hope this book will help in your choice of the "next step." Maybe you will decide that doubts about going to college right after high school are unfounded, and you are just going through the normal jitters before a new event. That's terrific. For you, sticking to the traditional path is the right choice.

But perhaps you will encounter people and ideas in this book that will make you think, "Hey! That's just the way I see things. If someone else did that, so can I." That's just great. You will have made the right decision, too.

The truth is, there is no one right way to grow up. And there is no way anyone can predict what the future holds for you. We are experiencing some of the most dramatic changes in this world since the Industrial Revolution. You are lucky to be on the cutting edge of the most exciting century ever. But you have to be prepared to try more things and take more risks than others who have come before you. Don't fret over little mistakes. They help you grow. Learn to listen to that inner voice that is always with you. If you think you are doing what's best for you, you probably are. Conversely, if your heart quickens because what you are about to do seems wrong, step back and take a long, hard look at what you've chosen. You may want to change directions.

You can't stop change from happening any more than you can stop yourself from growing up. (That is, in fact, the answer to the question, "Do I have to grow up?")

The best of luck in whatever you choose. And remember, plan to have a lot of fun along the way.

Chapter 1

Who Am I?
Why Am I on This Planet?

RIGHT NOW YOU ARE SUPPOSED TO BE HAVING THE TIME OF YOUR LIFE. Isn't that what all the adults are telling you? After all, besides being in the bloom of youth, you are coming of age during the morning of a new century—the Information Age. (Virtually anyone who was your age at the turn of the last century is long dead, but they must have felt the excitement you are feeling now.) All kinds of new possibilities will be open to you—so many, in fact, that it's hard to figure out where to begin.

Are you someone who thinks that if only you could figure out what you want to do, you'd go ahead and do it? Or do you know exactly what you want but feel as if you are drowning in a sea of boredom? If a good fairy could grant you one wish, would it be that you would be someplace where you are intellectually challenged—someplace where other kids would know what you are talking about? Or better yet, understand your jokes?

Ever since junior high school, teachers and parents have been exhorting you to plan for your future. But how can you plan for the future if you haven't a clue about what you want or can do? How can you find out what's out there in the world for you? How do people figure out their life's work, anyway? And will you have to do the same work your whole life?

Sometimes it's hard enough to plan what to do on Saturday night, let alone for the rest of your life. Other times, it's easier to sketch out the big picture, but it's impossible to decide which college you might want to attend, which subjects you'd like to study, or even if college is the right choice. Or you may be thinking, "Do I really have to go to college at all, when all I want to do is travel? Or get a job so I can finally earn some money and be on my own?" Or "Why can't I go to college right now, since there isn't anything left for me to take in high school?"

And then there is the enormous sum of money that college costs these days. Somehow the idea of being deep in debt at age 22 isn't exactly what you had in mind as a way to begin your adult working life. And sticking your parents with your college debt when they might have other kids to put through college could put them in hock for the rest of their lives! Yet if you don't go to college—or get postsecondary education or training in a trade—your chances of earning a good living in the Information Age are pretty slim.

What do people mean when they say these are the best years of your life? The most confusing years are more like it.

Your parents tell you that you have to go to college, but it will probably bankrupt them.

Your teachers tell you that without an education you'll never earn enough money to support yourself.

Your music tells you that the most important thing in life is falling in love.

Your friends tell you to live for the moment.

And inside of you a small voice is saying, "Hey! Stop the world. I want to get off."

Don't panic.

Other kids have felt the way you do right now. (In fact, so did your parents and teachers when they were your age.) Most of us manage to grow up and find work we love or at least like. The journey may seem hit-and-miss, but every time you try something new, you add to your store of life skills.

Now is the time to investigate a whole range of options before deciding what to do after high school. You might travel to a foreign country, where you can meet people and learn a new language, do a summer internship in a field that interests you, work with a disadvantaged population, gain solid work skills, earn money toward your college education, volunteer for a nonprofit organization, or test yourself in an Outward Bound program. If you are willing to try some things that are off the beaten path, you will have the opportunity to grow in ways you never thought possible.

Chris Batt, from Wilmington, Delaware, dutifully went off to college after he finished high school but really couldn't figure out why he was there. He decided to work for a while in a sporting-goods store. In his spare time he coached crew (rowing) for inner-city youth. In the back of his mind, he dreamed of a career in television. When a college counselor suggested he take part in an

Dynamy interns working on a TV documentary for the Worcester State Audio Visual Department. (Author's collection)

internship program called Dynamy, Inc., in Worcester, Massachusetts, Chris got a chance to work at local TV channel WGMC, where he and other interns got to "do everything." Chris learned that internships are invaluable in helping a person figure out the "next step."

The day Lucy Morris's grandmother took her to Sugarbush Airport near Montpelier, Vermont, when she was 14, Lucy knew she wanted to fly. She fulfilled that dream at 18. Then she had to figure out how she could earn a living flying. Later, with her college degree in flight management, Lucy found flight instructor opportunities somewhat limited. But today, at 24, she is looking forward to a hitch with the Coast Guard, hoping that she will be given the kind of responsibility she craves.

"With my flight management degree, the Coast Guard will probably give me more responsibility sooner than, say, some of the 18-year-olds who joined up when I did. I don't know what's in store for me, but I'm excited," Lucy said when she'd finished her basic training and was waiting for her first ship assignment.

William Glass lived in a small village in upstate New York and had taken all of the advanced placement math and science courses offered at his high school by the time he was finished with his freshman year. He knew he was ready for college. "But I didn't want to go to a university, where I'd just be mixed in with everybody else," he says. He applied to and was accepted at the Clarkson School in Potsdam, New York. Clarkson provided Will with a one-year "bridge" program. He lived and studied with other students like himself in a dorm set aside for them on the Clarkson campus. He took regular classes at Clarkson University. At the end of the year, he had a year's worth of valuable college credits and was ready to transfer to M.I.T. The Clarkson School was, Will says, "the first real academic challenge I'd had."

John Weeldreyer of Chapel Hill, North Carolina, just couldn't figure out what it was he wanted to do after high school, but he knew he needed to get himself organized. "I didn't want to go to college. I didn't have money or parental support at that time." He checked out the possibilities in the armed forces and decided to join the Navy for two years. "It was the best thing I ever did for myself," John says.

Chris Biacioni of Ithaca, New York, had studied Spanish for all four years of high school but wanted to be totally fluent before she went off to college. "And," she says, "I wanted some time away from my family so that I could grow up. I want to feel as though I can take care of myself." She applied to her local Rotary International Club to spend a year in Mexico. Chris's family hosted a Rotary student from the Netherlands during her senior year, and they became great friends. Now Chris looks forward to living with a Mexican family. It doesn't matter to her that most of her friends will be going off to college or that she'll be doing an extra year of high school in a foreign language and in another country. This will be a year for her to fulfill one of her dreams.

> "I wanted some time away from my family so that I could grow up."

How are you going to figure out if you're the kind of person who will be making the right choice if you do the traditional thing: high school, college, career, and maybe graduate or professional school sandwiched in there somewhere?

How will you know if you decide to go to college a year or two early that you won't be giving up the best part of high school and growing up too fast—or, worse yet, that you aren't really emotionally ready to accept the challenge of college?

If you decide to postpone college for a couple of years, or stop out after a year or so into college, how can you know that you will return to complete your education? Maybe after a year or more away from the books, you won't remember how to study—or want to. And if you do put off college for a year or two, won't you feel that you are too old to be just starting college? What will happen if you decide to stop out for work or travel and you can't find a job or your travel plans fall through? Or maybe college isn't really important at all. It's all so confusing—isn't there someplace to get some facts?

WHERE TO GET RELIABLE INFORMATION

The U.S. Department of Labor tracks the employment and earning possibilities for high school graduates compared with college graduates. Three things stand out:

First, the more you learn, the more you earn. For the first four months of 2003, the U.S. Department of Labor surveyed workers ages 25 to 34. The median wage for someone *without* a high school diploma was $21,400. For a *high school graduate,* it was $28,000. For a person with *some college* but no degree, median earnings were $32,400. The median salary jumps to $35,400 for a person with an *associate degree* from a two-year college. A *bachelor's degree* increases one's earnings to a median of $46,300, and with a *master's degree,* salaries jump another $11,000 to 56,300. (Median income is the midpoint of a set of figures with an equal number of data above and below the median.)

Second, the unemployment rates are equally impressive. Slightly over 3 percent of people *with* college degrees in the same age group were unemployed during this period. With *some* college, the rate is still relatively low—between 4.6 percent and 4.8 percent. A *high school graduate* with no further training faced an unemployment rate of between 5.4 percent and 6.0 percent, and *without a high school diploma,* a person faced the highest unemployment rate of between 8.2 percent and 9.0 percent.

Third, there's more bad news for people without a college education. The number of jobs that don't require a college diploma is shrinking—even jobs that formerly required no more than a high school diploma now want workers who have had some college. Many factory jobs that used to pay good wages are either in decline or being moved to foreign countries, where there is a ready supply of cheaper labor. However, there are many opportunities for people who have not gone to college but who go into certain trades. There are excellent job prospects for men and women who train to become auto-, motorcyle-, or boat-maintenance mechanics; electricians; carpenters; plumbers; beauticians; and other skilled workers. Many employers report that there is a lack of qualified workers to fill these jobs. To find out what you can earn in one of these trades in any city in the United States, check out http://swz-hotjobs.salary.com.

WHAT SKILLS WILL YOU NEED?

Peter Francese, founder of *American Demographics Magazine,* which is read by people who work in government, business, and academia all over the English-speaking world, carefully studies reports put out by the U.S. Department of Labor and other government agencies. As the title of this magazine suggests, Mr. Francese is especially interested in population figures and reports on how shifting populations influence the job market. He and the magazine's editors use the information gained from a variety of government sources to make predictions about job growth and decline in specific areas. Mr. Francese is able to identify the skills that will help you succeed in this global-information-hungry age.

"The first of these," he says, "is the ability to write very well." There are many different kinds of writing skills, he notes. One particularly useful skill is to be able to look at a set of facts and describe them. "But the ability to look at a set of facts and tell a story . . . is an enormously valuable skill. . . . That kind of skill takes years to learn, and it is not something that is right or wrong. It is a skill which is continually updated."

The second is "the ability to communicate verbally with people, to be persuasive, and to be convincing in terms of your point of view. So much of what is done in business and education and health care today is done in meetings and is done with people who . . . pool their knowledge and use the combined information to solve a problem," says Francese.

One skill everyone should have, no matter what you do, says Mr. Francese, is typing. He also recommends that you learn a second language. "It almost doesn't matter which language, but my personal preference is Spanish. But people who can write and speak Chinese or Japanese are just immensely in demand. Such a person can make anywhere from 50 to 100 percent more on a regular basis than a person who speaks only one language."

Learn how to manage yourself! "The ability to make intelligent choices about how to spend one's time and [know] what sorts of activities are going to be beneficial . . . will keep you healthy and competitive with others."

And finally, Mr. Francese says it's important to learn how to manage others. "People who can manage human resources [other people] are more valuable than people who can't."

WHERE ARE THE JOBS?

Based on U.S. Department of Labor statistics and other sources, Mr. Francese identifies three major areas with enormous growth and a variety of job opportunities within each field. These are health care, education, and information services.

1. Health care, Mr. Francese notes, is "a trillion-dollar industry." He points out that our population is aging in a very specif-

ic manner. "In the next decade the fastest-growing age group will be people in their fifties. And around the age of 50 people begin to become afflicted with chronic things like diabetes, high blood pressure, and other such things, as well as general wear and tear on the body." There are literally tens of millions of aging baby boomers, and they will need all kinds of medical attention and a variety of traditional and nontraditional therapies.

In addition to the aging boomers, people over 85 will number between three and five million. They will require home health care and care in a variety of nursing home facilities.

Of course, as we move into the second decade of the twenty-first century, there will be another population shift. Health care will continue to be a growing industry, not just in providing care but also in the areas of providing information, record keeping, and basic scientific research.

2. Education is the second growth industry. Mr. Francese finds that there will be a "clump" of teens moving into the late teen and early adult bracket. There will be a 16 percent growth in this age group—fron 25 million to 29 million. The demand for teachers at all levels will increase, as will the demand for people who can create educational materials, including educational software, CD-ROMs, and other materials that help people learn in a "computerized environment."

3. Information processing is the third area of growth. "There is," says Mr. Francese, "an absolute explosion in the number of firms that provide geographic data," as well as environmental data, consumer information, and natural-resource management, among other areas. "There are immense opportunities in the area of information processing . . . and any young person who has the natural facility for analysis of numerical information has a very bright future."

In addition, there are many trades that have a bright future for an ambitious person who likes to work with his or her hands and is willing to work hard.

ALL THERE IS, IS CHANGE. NO CHANGE=NO LIFE!

Whether we realize it or not, we all build on the skills we already have. Even if you think you don't know very much right now, you know more than you think. You may be great in math, computers, or music. You may excel in language or in simply getting people to cooperate with each other. You may already have a burning interest in politics or biology or bicycles or earthworms. Or you may be a science fiction buff or someone who held a part-time job after school at a tofu factory. The idea is that there are things you already know, and things you may want to learn later, and things you haven't yet thought about learning.

> "Knowing yourself, your talents and capabilities, will help you move on."

In this great new Information Age, you will be expected to accept change, to try new things, and to adapt to new situations. Whether you feel excited, terrified, or indifferent about change doesn't matter. Knowing yourself, your talents and capabilities, will help you move on. And although you "may not be sure of what it is you want to do, or even what's out there for you, it's important to keep your options open," says Dr. George Conneman, retired director of instruction at the College of Agriculture and Life Sciences at Cornell University.

There's no better time than right now to start thinking about what's special about yourself.

KNOW THYSELF

Here is a test you may want to try. (See page 14.) Actually, it isn't really a test. It's a tool to help you create a picture of yourself. There are no wrong or right answers to any of the questions. And there are no trick questions. Since you don't keep score, you can't flunk. But do make the answers your own rather than what you think somebody else thinks you should be doing.

This isn't even one of those tests that is supposed to tell you what you should be when you grow up. What you may get, however, are some clues about the direction you can take over the next couple of years.

The items on the test represent a variety of skills, attitudes, personal qualities, information, and understandings you may or may not have—or want to have. All the items included here have been found at some time, in some place, to be valuable in the adult world. No one, regardless of age or achievement, would be likely to rank at the high end for every item.

You are invited to think about your skills and your personal development. Consider what you believe you are good at, and think about whether or not you want to put your energy into improving in some weak areas over the next year or so, or in using your strengths in a new way.

> "There's no better time than right now to start thinking about what's special about yourself."

The idea for this self-assessment test came from Joan Webster, who for many years taught and counseled students at Vermont College. She developed her test for people who were starting college as older students. Many of them had been homemakers and parents. Other had worked in factories and on farms. Most were unsure of their skills and had doubts about their ability to perform in a college setting. Ms. Webster found that this kind of test helped them sort things out. Together, Ms. Webster and I revised the test so that it can help you think through your own development as a young person on the brink of adulthood.

You may want to assess yourself more than once. It's a good idea to make several copies of the test before marking it up. If you copy it on several sheets of different colored paper, it may help when you go back to check yourself.

Try the test now, and after you've had a chance to think about it, put it away in a drawer. In a couple of months, after you've made some decisions about your future plans and have been engaged in them for a while, take the test again. You will be amazed at how many new skills you've acquired and how many of your attitudes have changed. Study the results carefully. They will help you create a picture of yourself that will help you move into the adult world.

> **"You may want to assess yourself more than once."**

Of course, there are many other kinds of aptitude tests given by educational professionals. A good test may help you sort out what professions might be right for you. Many tests are based on the special interests and skills of successful lawyers, teachers, scientists, etc. The theory is that certain people with the same personality traits tend to do well in certain careers.

However, even if it turns out that you share the same traits as successful surgeons, if you can't stand the sight of blood, you'd probably do well to stay away from surgery, but you might consider other careers in the medical field.

There are many tests geared to helping you define your choices. The Strong-Campbell Inventory Test measures your interests against 100 people who are happy and successful in a variety of careers. There's SIGI—a computerized values-clarification test—the Jackson Vocational Interest Survey, and the Kuder Preference Record, which measures occupational interests, to name just a few. Your high school guidance counselor, an educational consultant, or a college career officer can tell you where you can take these tests if you are interested in finding out more.

> "No one test, however, can hold all the answers for you. You need to follow what is in your heart."

No one test, however, can hold all the answers for you. You need to follow what is in your heart.

SELF-ASSESSMENT

Name [   ]   **Date** [   ]

For each item, show your judgment of yourself by filling in spaces to create a bar. You may stop at any bar anywhere between low and high.

	LOW	**HIGH**

Writing ability

For example, for the skill "Writing Ability," here's how you might fill in the boxes:

	LOW	**HIGH**

Writing ability

"Writing is something I don't do well."

OR...

Writing ability

"My writing isn't horrible, but it isn't great."

OR...

Writing ability

"My writing ability is all right but could be better."

OR...

Writing ability

"Writing is something I do very well."

PART I: GENERAL ACADEMIC SKILLS

LOW   **HIGH**

Writing ability

Reading comprehension

Ability to express
ideas orally

Ability to understand
what others say

Ability to ask questions

Ability to seek and try
solutions to problems

Ability to solve complex
mathematical problems

Ability to do everyday
mathematical problems

Ability to concentrate on
difficult reading material

Ability to formulate questions

Ability to seek out teachers
and other experts to help
clarify difficult material

Ability to work
independently in library

Ability to study with
other students

Ability to study difficult
material alone

Ability to complete
schoolwork on time

Ability to complete
assignments in subjects
that are least liked

Ability to become absorbed
in a new subject

Ability to share ideas with
classmates

PART II: PERSONAL AND INTERPERSONAL ATTITUDES AND QUALITIES

PERSONAL	LOW	HIGH

Self-confidence

Physical fitness

Ability to set short-term
personal goals

List three short-term goals, if possible:

1.

2.

3.

Ability to set long-term
personal goals

List three long-term goals, if possible:

1.

2.

3.

Tolerance for frustration

Development of a
personal value system

Indicate what you value most, if possible:

1.

2.

3.

Ability to finish projects
you initiate

Ability to work without
supervision

Ability to be alone

Willingness to try something
physically demanding

Willingness to change plans
for a new challenge

Willingness to learn new tasks

Ability to take criticism

Willingness to take a
calculated risk

Ability to receive compliments

Willingness to be innovative

Willingness to challenge yourself

Ability to act on intuition

Ability to appreciate your
own strengths

Ability to like yourself

Ability to bounce back after
you have been criticized

Ability to laugh at yourself

Ability to make use of leisure time

Ability to develop new hobbies ▮▮▮▮▮▮▮▮▮▮▮▮▮▮▮▮▮▮▮▮

INTERPERSONAL **LOW** **HIGH**

Ability to work with peers ▮▮▮▮▮▮▮▮▮▮▮▮▮▮▮▮▮▮▮▮

Ability to work with older
people ▮▮▮▮▮▮▮▮▮▮▮▮▮▮▮▮▮▮▮▮

Ability to adapt to new
situations ▮▮▮▮▮▮▮▮▮▮▮▮▮▮▮▮▮▮▮▮

Ability to get along with
different kinds of people who
are of the same age ▮▮▮▮▮▮▮▮▮▮▮▮▮▮▮▮▮▮▮▮

Ability to get along with
older people ▮▮▮▮▮▮▮▮▮▮▮▮▮▮▮▮▮▮▮▮

Ability to fit in with new
social situations ▮▮▮▮▮▮▮▮▮▮▮▮▮▮▮▮▮▮▮▮

Willingness to take orders
from someone who may not
be as smart as you are ▮▮▮▮▮▮▮▮▮▮▮▮▮▮▮▮▮▮▮▮

Ability to do a boring or
unpleasant task for pay ▮▮▮▮▮▮▮▮▮▮▮▮▮▮▮▮▮▮▮▮

Willingness to learn new tasks ▮▮▮▮▮▮▮▮▮▮▮▮▮▮▮▮▮▮▮▮

Ability to make the best of things ▮▮▮▮▮▮▮▮▮▮▮▮▮▮▮▮▮▮▮▮

Willingness to stick to your
guns when you're convinced
you're right ▮▮▮▮▮▮▮▮▮▮▮▮▮▮▮▮▮▮▮▮

INFORMATION & SKILLS **LOW** **HIGH**

Acquisition of specific
information or skills ▮▮▮▮▮▮▮▮▮▮▮▮▮▮▮▮▮▮▮▮

Name your special interests:

1.

2.

3.

INFORMATION	LOW	HIGH

Knowledge of how city and county governments work

Knowledge of how state government works

Knowledge of local issues

Name specific issues of concern:

1.

2.

3.

Knowledge of national affairs

Name specific issues of concern:

1.

2.

3.

Knowledge of world affairs

Name specific issues of concern:

1.

2.

3.

Knowledge of history:

1. world

2. national

3. state

4. local

Understanding of other cultures

Specify, if possible:

1.

2.

3.

Understanding of how people
behave and why

Knowledge of the sciences

Name areas, if possible:

1.

2.

3.

Interest in exploring the arts
(art, music, drama, dance)

Name activities and forms:

1.

2.

3.

Knowledge of mathematics

Understanding of your
own past

Knowledge of world geography

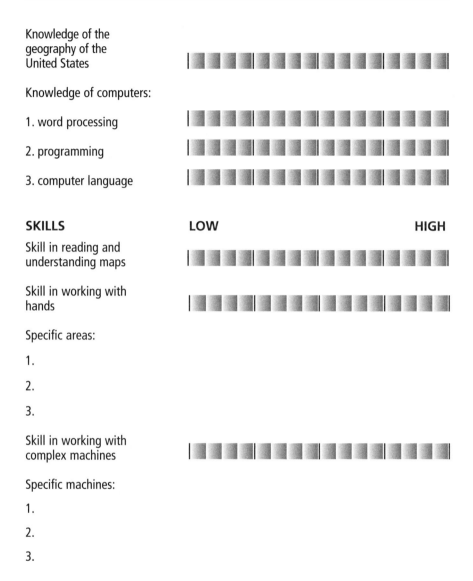

Knowledge of the
geography of the
United States

Knowledge of computers:

1. word processing

2. programming

3. computer language

SKILLS   **LOW**   **HIGH**

Skill in reading and
understanding maps

Skill in working with
hands

Specific areas:

1.

2.

3.

Skill in working with
complex machines

Specific machines:

1.

2.

3.

PART III: ANALYZING YOUR ANSWERS

1. What are the qualities and attitudes I identified as strongest in Part I?

2. Of these, which do I want to develop further?

3. Which things do I want to work on now, and which do I want to set aside for "someday"?

4. Which attitudes and qualities do I think will help me in planning my next step?

5. Of those areas which I want to develop further, which are for "someday" and which are for "now"?

When you have done more than one self-assessment, place the last two next to each other and ask yourself about the changes you see in your responses. Ask yourself, "How do I explain each difference? Was each the result of a plan, or did it just happen? What do I want to do next? What should I shelve for a later time?"

Take time to appreciate yourself before deciding what to do next, whether you are doing the assessment for the first time or comparing versions. The good thing is that you don't need to learn everything at once. You've got a whole lifetime ahead of you, and you will be learning all the time.

In the following chapters you will read about people your age whose choices about their immediate futures didn't exactly match what their friends were doing. As you read about what they did and how they did it, you may want to think how they would have responded to the self-assessment test you've just completed. And you may want to consider how you might feel attempting something a little off the beaten path.

Chapter II

Stopping Out: Is It Right for You?

SHOULD YOU PUT YOUR COLLEGE EDUCATION ON HOLD? For some, the answer may be a resounding yes. You may not, for example, be a particularly good student in high school. Do your teachers write "Does not live up to his/her potential" on your report card? Do you know you really could do A or B work if you actually did some studying? Do you feel you will be wasting your time if you go to college now? Or are you suffering from senior burnout and needing to relax and think about your goals for a while? Do you simply not have the money to pay for the college you really want to attend? Working and saving your money for a year or two could certainly help. Perhaps there are some things you'd like to do now, while you are young and have fewer responsibilities—travel, community service, or living in a foreign country, for example. The diverse reasons for stopping out, as you will see from the stories here, may strike a chord with you.

It's easy to make your friends believe that striking out in a direction different from what your parents expect is a sensible and sane idea. Convincing your parents and even your guidance counselor (to say nothing of your Uncle Manny, a nice guy who has been stuck in a dead-end job because he dropped out of high school years ago, and who thinks you'll wind up like him) may take some doing.

Who Stops Out?

➤ Those who need to raise money for college

➤ Students who take themselves seriously and are self-directed

➤ Students who have no real reason for being in college

➤ Independent-minded students who are not overly influenced by their peers

➤ Students for whom an unusual opportunity presents itself

➤ Outgoing high achievers who are risk-takers

➤ Students who have spent a year or two in college and need a break from academic life

➤ Students who need to prove to themselves that they can be independent

Deans of admissions at prestigious colleges and universities are generally enthusiastic about students who take time out between high school and college.

"It's a fine thing to do, and we will defer a student for a year," says Linda Miller, associate dean of admissions at the University of Virginia in Charlottesville. "However, we ask that the student submit a plan on how they expect to find themselves in some way. We want them to do something in a constructive way for a while."

Yet there are compelling arguments for going directly to college after high school:

➤ Going to college right after high school is the normal and traditional thing to do.

➤ Going to college right away allows a person to make realistic career plans.

➤ Entering college right after high school maintains the momentum of study habits.

➤ It is easier to make friends during freshman year when everybody is roughly the same age.

➤ Students who want to take a year out to work, study abroad, or do an internship are more likely to be accepted to competitive programs if they already have some college years behind them.

PARENTS NEED TO BE CONVINCED

If you can step away from yourself and your own problems for a moment and think about why your parents might not agree with your decision, you may be able to prove to your parents that you are mature enough to make this kind of decision. (Shouting "I'm 18 [or 16 or 17]. I'm old enough to make my own decisions," generally doesn't do much to prove your maturity.) Once you understand their concerns, you have a much better chance of marshaling your arguments and gaining parental approval. The more information you have before you bring up your plans, the better you'll be able to argue your case successfully. Once your parents understand that what you are doing is a positive action and not a negative one, they may even be pleased with your decision—or at least accept it.

WHO STOPS OUT AND WHY

"I was the bad kid"

Michael Urgo says, "I wasn't sure where I wanted to be and what I wanted to do. My freshman and

> "I wasn't sure where I wanted to be and what I wanted to do."

What Your Parents Might Say

➤ You will be wasting time.

➤ Everybody else is going to college, and you will lose all your friends.

➤ You may never go to college if you stop out.

➤ You won't learn anything of value by stopping out.

➤ You are too young to make that kind of decision.

➤ It will be too difficult to study after you've been away from school.

➤ Once you get to college, you'll be glad you listened to us.

➤ It's always been our dream to send you to college.

➤ If you stop out, you will lose your scholarship.

➤ Don't even think about it. You're going to college, and that's that.

sophomore year in high school were spent in [Washington] D.C., and I did miserably in school. I was kind of a bad kid and got sent to boarding school. I come from a family of 10 children—nine boys and one girl. And I was the only one sent away. I have four older brothers and they are all successful. And then there was me."

Even though Michael did all right at boarding school, he just couldn't decide on a college. "The applications would scare me. I didn't want to do it. I didn't want to go to school." Nevertheless, he wound up at a small all-male Southern college because he was offered a sports scholarship. "But there wasn't much to do there except drugs. So I got into that and I failed out of school and came back home." After going "through the motions" again at a local community college, Michael realized he was just wasting his time. And he wanted to get away.

"I knew I wanted to be on the West Coast," he says. So he tried to get a job in British Columbia through "something called Interwest." But when he arrived in Canada, Michael discovered the job didn't exist. "I was 19, and I didn't have a job, and I didn't want to leave. So I worked under the table. I'd save some money, and then I'd go rock climbing or kayaking or skiing. I was living an incredible life." But after six months, Michael knew he was just being irresponsible, and at his parents' insistence, he came back home. Still, Michael felt his time in British Columbia was important in terms of becoming "closer to the outdoors, and a kind of spirituality."

Time out to work on an organic farm

Pedro Magallanes Talamas is from Chihuahua, Mexico. He'd already finished two years of college, majoring in electrical engineering, when he decided to take time out to work on an experimental farm in Rutland, Massachusetts. Overlook Farm is part of an organization known as the Heifer Project International, a nonprofit organization that fights hunger in impoverished areas by providing livestock and training to small-scale farmers. There are three model farms in the United States. A family friend had spent a year at Overlook Farm.

"She told me about the farm and the fact that if I went there, I could improve my English. Before I went, I was just thinking of the new technology and the new computers or just what I like—cars, for example. But when I got to the farm and looked all day at nature, and worked with the farm animals and the crops, or when I was teaching people how to work with nails and a hammer—I wanted to change my major to work with animals or something like that."

For his work, Pedro received a modest living allowance of $200 monthly (currently, the stipend is closer to $300 monthly for those who stay more than three months), lived on the farm, and learned how to farm organically. "This farm tries to be 100 percent organic—all the vegetables are raised organically. We don't use any tractors; everything is done by hand. If you have to weed, you use your hands. And the animals—we didn't give them any feed that wasn't organic. All the products we sell— milk or meat or fruit and veggies—we can say that it's organic," says Pedro.

Heifer Project International trains people in impoverished areas "to work with animals and [shows them] how they can use all the products from the animal—milk, meat, eggs, etc.— so they can eat better and have a little left over. The Heifer Project doesn't give money; they give people training," Pedro says. They may provide a farmer with a cow, and when that cow produces a calf, the farmer gives it to a neighbor to raise, and that farmer will pass along the next offspring. More than 20,000

Pedro Magallanes Talamas demonstrates brick making to the homeschool campers at the Peru site of Overlook Farms. (Pedro Magallanes Talamas)

visitors come to Overlook Farm each year. There are model village homes and small farms there, so that people can experience what it would be like to live in a poor village in Peru or Thailand or Guatemala.

"This is the kind of training that can be used in Mexico," Pedro says. "I don't know why poor farmers would need a computer. The best way to help people is to do something that will help them feed their families and become independent."

The experience Pedro was most proud of was when he learned how to train water buffalo, which are used in Thailand. Not only are these animals huge, but they also have horns. "Almost everybody is afraid of them," says Pedro. "But I learned to control them first with a stick, and then with my voice. And," he says, "I have two scars on my body to prove it." If training the water buffalo was the best thing, the hardest time for Pedro was during his first two months on the farm, when two of the cows were pregnant. "They would not let you milk them. They would kick a lot, and we'd have to call [the man in charge of all the farm animals]."

In addition to working with the animals, Pedro did construction work and helped get the farm ready for spring planting. Other volunteers led tours of the farm and worked with visiting students and adults who would come for several days or a week to learn about the work of Heifer Project International.

Since he returned home, Pedro has had visits from several American friends he made on the farm. Now that he's finishing his degree, he's begun to think of ways to use that year's experience to improve the lives of those who live in the poor villages in his own country.

Overlook Farm accepts volunteers for varying amounts of time, from a month or two over the summer to six months or a year or longer.

Heifer Project International
Overlook Farm
216 Wachusett Street
Rutland, MA 01543-2099
(508) 866-2221
(508) 886-6729 (fax)
overlook.farm@heifer.org
http://www.heifer.org

A need to save for college

Aaron Seymour from Pittsfield, Massachusetts, was "into doing things with nature." The first year he was out of high school he heard about AmeriCorps, a nationwide program initiated by President Clinton in 1994. It is a national service movement that gives young people who are 18 or older the opportunity to do community service for up to two years (or in some cases, three years) in exchange for a modest living stipend plus money to either help pay off existing college loans or help finance college, graduate school, or vocational training in the future. Although Congress cut funding for a number of AmeriCorps programs in 2003, there are still many programs to choose from.

Aaron applied and was accepted to the Conservation Corps right in his own community. He worked a 30-hour week and was paid minimum wage. In addition, he received medical insurance and an education award of $4,725 for each year he successfully completed. And because Aaron was able to live at home, he saved a good part of his living stipend.

"We do things like brush cutting or helping the Massachusetts Audubon Society clean up the bird sanctuaries. We do painting and repairs to the senior citizens' home, which is run by the Massachusetts Public Housing Authority. I've also done some public service announcements on radio and TV on composting and recycling toxic waste products, with advice on how to properly dispose of car batteries."

A devastating accident didn't put his life on hold

When Trampas Strucker woke up after surgery his family were all standing around his bed. They were crying. "My dad [who is a physician] was trying to tell me that I couldn't ever again use my legs. I looked at him and said, 'Quit whining about what I can't do. I want to start concentrating on what I can do.' That was the first sentence out of my mouth [after the accident]."

After an incredibly successful rodeo where Trampas, who had been riding professionally since age 12, placed first in bareback riding in Vancouver, Canada, he and his riding partner drove back to Kasmir, Washington, where they met up with his partner's parents. "They were riding their Honda Goldman 1150, and we decided to switch and bring the bike home." With his partner in front and Trampas behind, the two boys pulled out and had gone less than half a mile on the highway when the kickstand hit the pavement. Trampas was thrown over the guardrail. "I was traveling about 45 miles per hour, and I hit hard enough for my spine to come up through my body and hit my sternum in two places. I totally shattered two discs, had 13 breaks in six ribs, plus multiple fractures in my right arm. And I stretched my spinal cord eight inches. When I first woke up I had minimal use of my arms and hand. Within four days [against all odds], I had total use of them."

> **"Quit whining about what I can't do. I want to start concentrating on what I can do."**

When the doctors at the University of Washington hospital told Trampas it would be six to nine months before he could leave the rehabilitation center, he said, "No way. I told them I'd be out of there in two, and they told me, 'No way.'" Three weeks later the doctors let Trampas attend the biggest rodeo in the state. He had already done the equivalent of three and a half months of rehab work. "My doctor let me go home for the stampede, and then I went back, and four weeks later I got released permanently. And I went back to high school and graduated with my class."

Despite the fact that he will never have use of his legs again, Trampas insisted on getting back into virtually all of the physical activities he'd been doing before the accident. "You know, I have this attitude that when anybody says I can't, I just say, 'I gotta try.' They said I'd never ride horses again, but within two or three months, I was riding horses every single day. And everybody said, 'Oh, you can't snow ski,' and I went ahead and now I snow ski. And a while ago, I wanted to get back to rock climbing, and everybody said, 'Oh, you can't rock climb.' I've been rock climbing all summer, enjoying it as much as I did before. It's all upper body. Ropes and upper body. I climbed for seven or eight years before I got hurt, since I was about 12. So I knew the fundamentals." He does allow that it is a "bit more difficult to do it without your legs."

> "You know, I have this attitude that when anybody says I can't, I just say, 'I gotta try.'"

It was right after he came back from his first rock climbing experience after the accident that he learned about AmeriCorps. Teachers and friends had told him about an opening that would allow Trampas to work with kids in the Ponasket School District.

"So," says Trampas, "I looked into it, got the paperwork done, and got the job."

The university of the road

"I was relieved [to finish high school]," said Sara Finegan, "and I wanted a break and wanted to learn more about the world. I had this picture of me traveling and learning more about the cultures of the world. So during the last semester of high school, I started to do some volunteer work with Earthwatch. It's kind of like eco-tourism. You help scientists in the field who are concerned with human health issues and ecology in virtually every part of the world."

The volunteer programs with Earthwatch are broken down into two-week periods. Sara's first experience took her to the Bahamas, where she met Ken Balcolmb and Diane Claredge, scientists who were running a dolphin survey for the Bahamian government. When Ken and Diane moved on to do a study with orca whales, they offered Sara an unpaid staff position helping with the photography. "I'd had some experience with photography at my school, so I fit right in." In addition to enjoying the work, Sara was able to get the science credit she needed to graduate from high school.

After graduation, Sara decided to go on another Earthwatch program in Malawi [in Africa] where scientists were studying humpback whales. In addition to sharpening her photography skills, she learned about marine mammology. "This was an incredible experience: to work with scientists and learn how data was collected and to help with the field survey and learn how field research was done."

By the time Sara returned from her third Earthwatch experien_ she still had the travel bug but decided that she really needed a way to earn some money before she could take off again_ a job in one of the local coffee shops, got herself an a_ soon learned that it wasn't easy to support herself on what she was paid. And she certainly wasn't able to save any money for travel.

So after a year or so, Sara decided two things: "I did want to go back to school, but I did want to travel, too. I wanted a trade that I could travel with."

Sara chose to enroll in The Finger Lakes School of Massage, where her mother was a teacher. It turned out to be an excellent choice. "I love the sciences, and I learned quite a bit about anatomy and the way the body works. The program ran from September to May, five days a week." At 19, Sara graduated from the school and got her New York State license to practice massage.

For a time she worked at a local spa, and later she worked on her own. "The money was excellent," she said, "and I felt that no matter what happens, I did have a trade, and I could make money."

But Sara was still antsy. She wanted to travel and she also wanted to go to college. So she did a little library research. She wanted to satisfy both desires. "I didn't want to sit in a classroom and have a professor telling me what was happening. I felt I needed to go and see this and learn this for myself." She found the Friends World Program (FWP), based at Long Island University. It's a program that encourages life experience, and has centers in different parts of the world. Through FWP Sara could travel and earn an undergraduate degree at the same time. And because she was given college credit for her experiences with Earthwatch and with the massage school, she was accepted as a sophomore. Before she knew it, Sara was off to London for her first semester.

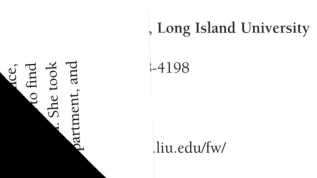

, Long Island University

-4198

.liu.edu/fw/

The Finger Lakes School of Massage
1251 Trumansburg Road
Ithaca, NY 14850
(607) 272-9024
(607) 272-4271 (fax)
admissions@flsm.com
http://www.flsm.com

The family rebel

By the time Matt Thomas graduated from high school, he'd been working full time for three years at a local restaurant. By his own admission, he was an extremely angry and rebellious teenager. At 14, he moved out of his mom's house to live with his dad. When that didn't work out, he moved out and tried to make it on his own. He cut school more often than not and soon wound up in trouble with the authorities after he and a friend were caught trying to break into a private home. A month's incarceration in a juvenile-detention center helped Matt understand that he had to stop lying, both to himself and others, in order to turn his life around. Then, with his parents' approval, he lived on his own while working and going to school.

"I was eager to grow up," he admits. "I wanted to prove I could support myself." Matt managed to graduate with a New York State Regents high school diploma while working full time in a restaurant.

For a while he flirted with the idea of enrolling in one of the prestigious culinary schools, but "I wasn't ready to take any kind of school seriously. I wanted hands-on experience in the restaurant business."

At 18 Matt had become the number-two person in the best French restaurant in town.

"Both the head chef and sous chef had quit in the same week, just seven months after I started working in this place," says

Matt, "and the owner hired a head chef and promoted me. I got a crash course in 'line cooking.'" But soon after his promotion, the restaurant burned down. Matt found other work until the restaurant was rebuilt. It reopened as a steak house, with Matt as sous chef.

Two years have passed, and Matt has begun to give his future some serious thought. He realized the only advancement he could make was as head chef, and that wasn't likely. Also, standing on his feet for eight or ten hours a night has had serious consequences. Matt has already had one operation on his knee.

Going to college to get an education began to look much more attractive.

As a first step, Matt has decided to update his math skills at the local community college so he can take the SATs. He has found other courses that interest him and has made the decision to become a full-time student.

"I'm ready to go back to school," he says. "But I'm not good enough yet for a four-year college, so I'm starting my education at the community college level, and I think I'm ready to work at my studies full time."

"I wanted to prove I could support myself."

Matt's parents are delighted. They have offered to pay his college expenses so that he won't have to continue working full time. "I'm not sure I like the idea of them supporting me, but I also know that I won't be able to do justice to my studies if I continue to work at the pace I'm doing now.

"You know, I was so eager to grow up fast, but now . . . I wouldn't mind some play time." At this juncture, going to college will allow Matt to have some "play time" along with some serious academic work.

"Not mature enough for college"

Nate Kipp from Cleveland, Ohio, was a student at Ohio Wesleyan University. "But I wasn't mature enough for college, and after my first year I was looking for something else to do."

At his father's suggestion, Nate attended a meeting of Habitat for Humanity, a program that helps people who can't otherwise own a home build affordable houses with volunteer labor and donated materials. Former United States President Jimmy Carter and his wife, Rosalynn, are major supporters of Habitat and often take up a hammer and saw to work alongside other volunteers. Generally, people do not get paid for volunteering for this organization, but it is now part of AmeriCorps and offers the same opportunity for qualified students as other AmeriCorps projects.

"It seemed like a pretty good thing," says Nate. "The first year I was in Homestead, Florida, where we built houses for people who had lost homes in the hurricane. We started on Jordan Commons, a 200-home project. We had a lot to do and were kept very busy." In addition to the unpaid volunteers, there were between ten and 20 AmeriCorps workers on the site.

> "You know, I was so eager to grow up fast, but now . . . I wouldn't mind some play time."

A plan to volunteer in an African nation

Sue Schwartz has always been active in her church and was a solid B student all through high school. She decided not to apply to college right away. What she wanted to do was to volunteer in Zimbabwe. "I had read *Cry, the Beloved Country* [a classic novel by

Alan Paton about racial inequality and injustice in South Africa]," she says, and it moved her. So Sue researched various organizations that have volunteers in Third World countries. She mailed dozens of applications. "I was really into saving the world," says Sue. "I wanted to check out the real world before going to college."

To Sue's dismay, she was rejected everywhere. No one seemed to want a high school graduate with few qualifications to volunteer in Africa.

She took a job at a local cafe and tried to save up some money while continuing her search. Finally she located a small nonprofit organization, Educate the Children, which runs education programs for poor children in Nepal. Two months later, Sue found herself in Katmandu, learning Nepali and teaching English in a small private school for lower caste children.

> "I wanted to check out the real world before going to college."

Time out for reflection

Leana Horowitz went to high school in Watkins Glen, New York. She'd spent her junior year of high school as a Rotary exchange student in Japan. It was during this year abroad that her mother first suggested she consider taking a year off after completing high school to reflect upon her Japanese experience.

"We corresponded frequently during that year, and gradually the idea took hold." Her father "thought that if I took a year off, I'd never go to college. But in my mind, that was never a problem. I love school."

Leana was accepted to Harvard University. There was a check box for deferred admission on the acceptance form. When Leana pointed this out to her dad, he relaxed a little. He realized that stopping out wasn't just a whim of Leana's. In fact, at some universities, as many as 10 percent of incoming freshmen opt to defer admission for a year or more. Once Leana was assured, in writing, that her financial aid package would not be changed (unless, of course, the family's income changed), she checked off the deferred admission box. Then she set about looking for a job.

Adventure beckons

Allison Novelly of Branford, Connecticut, was all set to go to Georgetown University. "I had my roommate. I had my food plan. I had everything, and I came home in the beginning of July and told my parents I wanted to do a semester at sea."

Allison had been involved in a program called Action Quest for a few summers. One summer she went to Fiji and the Galapagos Islands, and another summer she completed a rescue-diving course. It was then that her skipper encouraged Allison to consider taking time out before college to join the program known as Sea-mester. "She knew my personality and my love of sailing and thought it would be a really great program for me to go on."

Allison's parents thought so too, although there were some raised eyebrows from her high school friends. She'd been a day student at a very traditional boarding school where virtually everyone went right to college. Undaunted, she wrote to her college, Georgetown University, and explained what she wanted to do for a semester. Since Georgetown, unlike some other colleges, didn't admit freshmen during the spring semester, Allison had to defer for an entire year. She sketched out a plan that included some volunteer work for her second semester. And while all her friends headed off to college, she flew down to the British Virgin Islands to begin an 80-day voyage at sea.

Sea-mester Programs (experiential and educational semester voyages for high school graduates and college students)
P.O. Box 5477
Sarasota, Florida 34277
info@seamester.com
http://www.seamester.com

HOW TO KEEP YOUR OPTIONS OPEN

If you decide on the stop-out route, make sure you keep your options open. Even if college isn't a priority now, it almost surely will be in the future.

1. If you know you will go to college after you take your year (or two) off, apply to college before you stop out—if you know which college you really want to go to. If it is possible, try to lock in your financial-aid package. However, associate dean of admissions Linda Miller says that at UVA this isn't possible. "As far as scholarship money for the student who defers—we don't have merit scholarship funds. Our scholarships are all needs-based, and all financial aid has to be refiled every year." This is probably true for most colleges, but your chances are good that in a year or two you will still qualify for financial aid.

2. Some schools will not honor a deferment and will simply put you back in the pool of applicants the following year. You will have to decide if you are willing to risk the possibility of not getting into your first-choice college the next time around.

3. If the college says you will have to reapply after stopping out, find out what your chances of getting accepted will be. Keep records of all correspondence.

4. Keep your college informed about your plans. If you will be traveling, make sure there is some way for you to collect your mail. You don't want to miss deadlines just because nobody was around to pick up your mail.

5. If you decide not to apply to college right away, take the SAT or the ACT before you graduate from high school. If you don't do as well as you think you can, you will have a chance to take them again and you will know what to expect. Make certain your school file is up to date and accessible from your high school guidance department.

6. Keep abreast of deadlines if you intend to apply to college during the year you have stopped out. If you don't, you may find yourself out of school longer than you had planned.

7. Keep lines of communication open with your parents and friends.

A need to prove oneself

Doug Leonard from Northampton, Massachusetts, knew by the middle of his sophomore year in high school that he didn't want to go to college right away. At that stage of his life, school wasn't a high priority, and his grades often reflected his lack of interest.

"Actually," he admits, "I wanted to quit school altogether. I'd felt I'd had enough." His parents did not take kindly to this. They pointed out that quitting high school would have very serious consequences. "You'll be cutting yourself off from all kinds of jobs," they cautioned. "And if you do decide you ever want to go to college, you'll have a very hard time getting in without a high school diploma."

Of course, Doug knew his parents were right. But his desire to get away from school was so strong that he checked with his guidance counselor to find the quickest way to graduate. "I wanted time to think about who I really was and what I wanted to do with myself."

Once Doug figured out how to graduate a year early, he really put his mind to it. He took the SAT and was surprised to find that despite some problems with dyslexia, he'd scored quite well. That

> ## "I wanted time to think about who I really was and what I wanted to do with myself."

was important. First, it sent a signal to his parents that he was stopping out and not dropping out.

Second, Doug was keeping his options open. When he decided he was ready to apply to college, his test scores would be on file. Six months after he turned 16, Doug received his high school diploma and was eager to look for a job. "I wanted to prove that I could be something besides a student."

COMMON THREADS

If there is one thing these stories have in common, it is that regardless of what motivated these people to put their college education on hold, each one displayed an independent spirit. Even if some of them were not successful in gaining parental approval for their decisions, all tried to keep communication lines open. Says Leana, "Now that I've taken the year off, my dad talks it up with his friends who have college-bound kids." In fact, most of these parents finally agreed with their children's choices, especially when they saw that they were acting in responsible ways.

Chapter III

No More Pencils, No More Books: Work After School, or All That Glitters Is Hard to Get

I F YOU USE YOUR TIME AWAY FROM SCHOOL TO WORK, YOU CAN RUN INTO ALL KINDS OF PROBLEMS YOU NEVER DREAMED EXISTED. Leana remarks, "I'd never worked a forty-hour week before. It's a whole different world. School was fun. Work lasts from nine to five, and that's not always fun."

Sometimes the job that sounds great doesn't work out at all. The reasons may seem mysterious and frightening. As a first-time employee, you may not understand what's expected of you on the job, or you may find that you haven't thought through what you really want from your time out. Sometimes you and your employer simply won't get along, or perhaps there won't be enough work for you to do.

Problems may arise in the workplace, in your living situation, in how you use your free time, or in how you handle your money. Check back to see how you responded to some of the items in the self-assessment in Chapter I that have to do with short-term goals, ability to use leisure time, and ability to get along with people different from yourself. You may find that these are areas that are worth tracking even before difficulties arise. You probably won't be able to solve all your problems this way, but at least you may develop an understanding of why things can go wrong. As you read through the chapters that deal with working, you'll see how different people responded to difficult situations. Perhaps the coping strategies developed by others will work for you. Just being aware of potential trouble spots can be an advantage.

MAKE A PLAN

You're probably tired of everyone telling you to make a plan, but do it anyway. In fact, make lots of plans—before you finish high school, if possible. Then be ready to scrap or modify them as you gain new insights and experiences. Plans don't have to be elaborate, but they do have to be more complex than, "I plan not to have anything to do with school for one entire year." While getting away from school routines may be a driving factor in your stopping out, that in itself is not the plan. The plan will be what you do during that year or two.

You don't necessarily need a five-page, single-spaced, typeset of objectives and goals. You can make a plan for what you'd like to learn from a job or how much you expect to earn (and save) over the year. You can make a plan for how you will spend your earnings—what specific goodies you would like to own now that you will have your own money. You can plan to save for a trip or to put money away for college. You can make a plan for how you intend to spend your leisure time. Or, if you plan to do any traveling, when and where do you expect to go? The more thought you give to your time out, the more likely it is that you will be satisfied with what you've done. You are the only one of you there is, and if you don't take yourself seriously, no one else will either.

JOB OPTIONS

If you decide that at least part of your time out will be spent working, you need to figure out how to get a job when you may have no job experience. Most entry-level jobs aren't glamorous, and they don't pay very well. With a little luck, however, it won't take long to find your first job if you aren't picky. Even if the first job you get isn't what you want, you will learn something from it. Future employers will be impressed that you were able to work at even a dull job because it will show that you are a serious worker. There are also employers out there who are looking for people to train into responsible positions. So before you start job hunting, figure out what you want from your work experience.

1. Think about two or three areas in which you'd like to work and the reasons why.

2. Gather information. Check with family, friends, teachers, and guidance counselors to see if they can help you. If your best friend's mom says, "Oh, my brother-in-law owns a sporting-goods store. Would you like me to find out if he can use a stock person?" say yes if this is something you'd like. You'd be surprised how many people get jobs because they know someone who needs help.

3. Read the Help Wanted section of the newspaper every day, and look on the Internet for job advertisements and information about job hunting. Answer every ad that looks promising.

4. Register with the local State Employment Service. (It's in the white pages of the telephone book in your state's government section.) Once you register with the employment service, you will be allowed to log on to their database to find jobs that are listed with them.

5. Check out your local Youth Bureau, if your community has one. Often it has unusual jobs listed for young people.

6. Make a list of local businesses you are interested in working for. Do you know anyone who works there? If so, check to see if he or she will put in a good word for you. Are there businesses you

frequent? Do you know the boss? You can stop in and talk to him or her directly.

7. Phoning a place of business cold can be pretty scary, but you can also get lucky. So call first and ask for the name of the person in charge of hiring. Try to set up an interview.

8. Find out what kind of clothes are appropriate for the job and wear them for the interview. It is definitely a good idea to remove jewelry from your nose, lips, tongue, cheeks, etc. during interviews and during work. Spiked purple hair and torn jeans are not very likely to impress a prospective employer. But you already knew that, right?

9. Have a résumé ready to send to a prospective employer or bring one with you. Make certain that it is neatly typed and that there are absolutely NO TYPOS. Type it on a computer, and have it copied on good white or off-white paper (not in Day-Glo orange, please). In the world of work you need to impress employers with your ability to fit in, not stand out.

10. If you are told you will have to wait to find out if you are hired, keep looking for other jobs, but don't be afraid to check back. Persistence often pays off.

11. Tell everyone you know that you are job hunting.

12. It is better to be specific about the kind of job you are interested in. Telling a prospective employer you'll do anything means you haven't thought through your own specific skills or the kind of jobs the employer has to offer.

13. Look at job hunting as your job until someone hires you. That means you need to set up at least one job-search task for yourself every day. If you don't have an interview lined up, stop off at the employment service or a temp agency, browse a career Web site, or head for your library and read some books on how to conduct a job search.

14. Job hunting is exhausting—and sometimes filled with disappointment. Take time out to do something nice for yourself, or

for various neighbors—house painting, gardening. Again, don't pad this, but do include any paid work you have done. And if you have had experience in setting up a Web site for one of your parents or for a friend—or yourself—be sure to mention that.

The third section is where you can list your "ACTIVITIES." Have you done some community service work through your school, church, or synagogue? As a member of your school community, did you take part in any unusual activities, such as fund-raising to take a trip with your Spanish or French class to Mexico City or Paris? Did your bike group pedal 200 miles to the New Jersey Pine Barrens? Did you work with your school lunch program to get better food? Did you work on a special law project in your school? In other words, think about things that make you stand apart from other job applicants—and show that you will be a diligent worker.

Later on, as you build more job experience, get a college degree, and take part in internship programs, you will drop the stuff you did in high school from your résumé. For now, however, these things are important. One other thing: You may say, "References upon request." Before you give out the name of a person you wish to speak on your behalf, you must call that person and ask if you may use his or her name. Also, you will want to be sure that if you give a person's name to a prospective employer, that reference will say good things about you. You don't want a reference to say, "You want to hire Joe? I wouldn't do that! He did a terrible job on my garden last summer."

Keep a copy of your résumé on hand so that you can change and update it as you gain more experience. Every time you make a change, be sure to check your spelling.

MORE REASONS TO TAKE TIME OUT

There are many reasons to take a break between high school and college. Sometimes the decision is made for you.

Not accepted until spring semester

Leah Fagan was disappointed when Middlebury College wrote her that she'd been accepted for the spring semester and not the fall. Although she hadn't planned on taking time out, she recognized an opportunity when it landed in her lap.

"Inside the packet of material I was sent were suggestions of what to do in the semester before arriving on campus. They sort of expect you to be shocked that you're not going to be 'normal,'" she said. But the suggestions the college offered signaled her, and her fellow "Febs," that some "really cool things can happen during this semester."

There were suggestions for travel in the U.S. and abroad, suggestions for hooking up with classes at other colleges, and then, right at the bottom of the list, was a totally unique program. It was called "Ithaka," a semester spent on the island of Crete. "It was really different," said Leah, "and that above all else was exciting to me." Once she was accepted into the program, she flew to Athens and from there took another plane to Crete.

"There were 14 kids including me in the program, plus three tutors who lived with us 24/7, plus the director and five teachers for the 14 of us, plus the cook. They were always around, and you couldn't ask for better support." Besides learning Greek and the archeology, history, and literature of the area, each student worked every morning at an internship with a family from the village, and since most of the villagers didn't speak English, "we all learned to speak a little Greek, just by virtue of the fact that if we wanted to communicate, we needed to learn the language."

What sets this program apart from other study-abroad programs is that the students become a part of village life through the internships they undertake during the first part of each day.

Ithaka (a cultural study semester in Greece on the island of Crete)
5500 Prytania Street #102
New Orleans, LA 70115
(504) 269-2303
(504) 269-2301 (fax)
info@ithakasemester.org
http://www.ithakasemester.org

A plan that evolves

Philip Bereaud of Danby, New York, decided not to make a plan when he finished high school. "I thought I'd be too much like everyone else," he says. So at first he lived in his father's house until he found a job as a dishwasher in a local restaurant. As soon as he could, he moved into an apartment with a couple of older guys. "And then," he says, "I realized that my life was just as much a routine as when I was in school. It was just a different routine."

When a friend mentioned he was driving out to Oregon, Philip jumped at the opportunity to join him. While this seemed like a pretty irresponsible thing to do, Philip's real plan over the next two years grew out of his willingness to take chances and leave himself open to all kinds of new ideas.

Once Philip was in Oregon, he attended the trial of some social activists. Among those on trial was his traveling companion, Tim. There were 13 people—all part of a group called the Cathedral Force Action Group—on trial. They'd been arrested because they tried to prevent a logging company from cutting down the old growth trees (known as "cathedral trees") in a national forest.

"There was such a range of people on trial," Philip says. "Some were like Tim, who is a real hippie, and there were people who were clean-shaven and in suits. There were those who looked really wise—a whole variety of people."

The trial made Philip think that if people were willing to risk jail for the sake of trees, there must be something to what they were doing. None of the 13 was given a jail sentence. All were given probation.

Philip wanted to find out more. He decided to learn firsthand about the problems we are facing in our environment. Without realizing it, Philip was developing a plan for himself.

He joined a group called EarthFirst!. With about 200 others, Philip helped set up a camp in the woods in an effort to save a wilderness area called Oak Flats. Their goal was to draw attention to the problem of the diminishing national forests.

Philip says, "This is our land, and unless the public knows what's happening to it, the balance between timber, wildlife, and recreation and research will be destroyed." The camp attracted a lot of media attention—something that environmentalists know is important to their cause.

When the camp closed, Philip signed up to harvest fir cones. Just as he was finishing this job, he learned that there were dangerous forest fires to the south. He joined the firefighters who were putting out the fires among smoldering stumps. "We had to dig up the stumps and grind out the fires for 12 hours a day," he says.

Through these diverse experiences, Philip learned to get along with and understand the viewpoints of two completely different groups of people. When he was with the environmental group, he was associating with those who wished to be at one with the Earth and take as little as possible from it. When he was with the cone pickers and firefighters, Philip worked with those who saw the woods as a place to make money.

"At first I couldn't understand how a person could look at a tree and see money. But I learned when I was cone picking to look at a tree and say, 'Well, five bushels of cones are in that tree. It's a $50 tree.' And that's the way loggers do it. They look at a tree and say, 'Oh, that tree is so many board feet.'"

Not all plans work out

Remember Sue Schwartz from Chapter II? She wanted very much to volunteer in Zimbabwe but kept getting turned down. Although she tried to keep her spirits up during the first five months by working, it was a pretty discouraging time.

When the chance to go to Nepal arrived, she grabbed it. Sue's experience in Nepal turned out to be less than she had hoped. Part of it, she says, was her own lack of preparation. "I didn't do much research before I went to Nepal. I was very idealistic. I was just 17 at the time and really believed that I could change the world." On balance, however, Sue felt her five months in Nepal had their good points. "I taught English as a second language, I worked on a kindergarten project that Educate the Children was doing, and I worked in the villages, too." But Educate the Children is a very small operation. Sue realized that students volunteering through larger organizations had opportunities that were not available to her. The larger organizations arranged for their volunteers to meet interesting people who were working on diverse projects. "Everything that happened to me, I did for myself."

Sue also learned some lessons about development work in Third World countries. "I was disillusioned for quite a while because so much foreign money is wasted. I was upset because people in the United States don't think in broader terms about their own way of living. I went to Nepal to learn how to help people—to learn what's right and what's wrong, what's condescending and what's not."

Over the five months she spent in Nepal, Sue wrote to her parents many letters. She also kept a journal. When she came back to the United States, she was able to use one of the letters she wrote home as part of a college admission essay.

DEALING WITH REAL LIFE PROBLEMS

One of the first things you learn when you decide to take time out to work is that while all your friends have left for college, you are really on your own. You may seriously wonder if you haven't made a huge mistake. While school was a place where you made friends, the workplace is where you are expected to work, not socialize. Of course, you will get two 15-minute breaks as well as a half hour

Keeping Old Friends, Making New Ones

No matter how happy you are not to go off to college, it can be pretty depressing to watch your friends leave for someplace that promises to be exciting. Here are some tips from those who have been there.

➢ Don't lose contact with your old friends. Even if they go away to college, keep up a correspondence via e-mail, letters, or phone.

➢ Plan visits with special friends at college.

➢ If you are staying in your hometown, join at least one organization in your community that has regular meetings.

➢ Take part in church or other group activities that are fun.

➢ Become a Big Brother or Big Sister to an elementary school kid.

➢ During the times you are really lonely, do something special for yourself.

➢ Remember that when you are on the job, you are being paid to work, no matter how small your salary. Keep your socializing to a minimum. If you do make friends on the job, consider it a bonus.

➢ In the beginning, be a keen observer of how your coworkers relate to one another.

for lunch, but even then you may not find your coworkers especially friendly.

Making new friends

Leana commented that all of her good friends were away at college. During her year out she worried that she was missing out on something. Doug thought that one of the worst things about the two years he stopped out was, "I didn't meet anyone. I made no friends of lasting quality. It was a lonely time. I'm a person who needed to work in a public place and be around people. I missed making friends. My old high school friends were making new friends [at college], while I was in a rut."

Not everyone experiences a lack of friends. Matt had a lot of friends who had either dropped out of high school or didn't want to go to college. "People just sort of hung out together," he says. For years, work was the most important thing in Matt's life. "I was so eager to get into the rat race." Gradually, however, as Matt progressed about as far as he could go in the restaurant business, the pals he'd hung out with became less interesting to him.

GETTING FIRED—WHEN TO QUIT

In the real world, lots of people get fired or laid off from their jobs. Anyone who shows up for work on Friday, only to be told it will be his or her last day, goes home angry and depressed. Even when the boss assures you it isn't your fault, or even when you didn't like the job in the first place, getting fired is a definite downer. You will want to leave the workplace quickly (after picking up your last paycheck). The last thing in the world you need is for your coworkers to see you in a shaken state.

You may not feel like telling your parents or your friends that you lost your job. But actually, you will feel better almost immediately when you do. For one thing, virtually anyone who has ever worked has gotten fired. By discussing your situation with people close to you, you will soon realize that getting fired is not a tragedy. It is simply a glitch in your plans. It doesn't mean you are a failure. It does mean, however, that you will have to look for a new job. It is sort of like falling off a horse or your bicycle. The sooner you get back on, the stronger you'll be. But before you start job hunting, you may want to rethink your work goals so you don't wind up in a similar situation.

Back on the street

Shortly after he started working as a dishwasher at a local restaurant, Doug was laid off. "That was a hard thing," he says. At 16 finding a job hadn't been easy, and working made him feel great. "I wasn't fired for being inefficient or indifferent. I was laid off because the manager had overhired." Still, it hurt. Nevertheless, he learned that even a little experience was enough to land him a job in a better restaurant. A few months later, however, he realized that this wasn't where he wanted to be. But Doug also learned that he couldn't just walk away from a job because he'd had a bad day.

"There was one moment that I recall as a striking means of growing up. It was a hard day, and I was exhausted. I was angry at the boss and the people I was working with. I wanted to quit. Suddenly, I realized that if I quit, I wouldn't eat. I probably could have gotten money from my parents; I knew I didn't want to do that. I couldn't quit for my own peace of mind.

"That was a specific moment in my life. And it was a very powerful experience."

Not long after this bad day, Doug landed a more satisfying job as a mechanic in the bicycle shop where he had bought all of his bike equipment since he was a little kid. He was able to convince the owner to hire him because he showed him that he had kept a job—even one he didn't especially like. He worked at the bicycle

If You Lose Your Job

➤ According to Richard Nelson Bolles, author of *What Color Is Your Parachute?*, losing a job is part of the real world. He says that the average worker has to job hunt at least eight times during his or her lifetime. And that estimate is for people who are building careers, not for teenagers looking for work!

➤ Sometimes there is no rhyme or reason for why you lose a job.

➤ If you have worked at a job for at least three months (even part-time), check with your state unemployment agency to see if you are eligible for unemployment insurance benefits while you are in between jobs.

➤ Try to maintain an optimistic attitude while you are job hunting.

➤ Try to find at least one person who will give you a good reference from your last job.

➤ Think about the kinds of jobs that may offer you a challenge.

➤ Make looking for a new job a top priority, and job hunt every single weekday. But remember, no one can job hunt for eight hours a day.

➤ If you are worried about money, work for a temporary agency for a couple of days a week until you land the job you want. Often a temp job can turn into a full-time one. Temporary agencies can be found in the Yellow Pages of the phone book under "Employment Agencies," in the Help Wanted pages of your newspaper, and on the Internet.

shop until he went off to college and then got hired back during summer breaks.

Matt got fired from a restaurant job he'd planned on quitting anyway. "The boss and I had a personality conflict, and I had already lined up another job, but not for another two weeks. But I was relieved when she fired me—although, of course, I'd rather have had the extra two weeks' pay and the chance to quit first."

Leana also got fired from her first job, as a bagger in a supermarket. "Even when it's a job you don't like, you are hurt when the boss fires you," she says. But that experience made Leana realize that it was important to look for work that offered her a challenge. She reviewed her reasons for stopping out and used her knowledge of Japanese to land a job in a Buddhist publishing firm in a nearby town. "I did everything—running accounts, bookkeeping, and shipping. I loved being around books and got along well with the woman I was working for. Even though I only got minimum wage, it was an excellent experience."

Am I Having Fun Yet? Nuts and Bolts of Making the Most of Your Time Out

WHOSE MONEY IS IT, ANYWAY?

OK, you've got that job. It looks as if things are really going according to plan. Gosh, though, the paycheck is smaller than you thought it was going to be.

How come? Well, along with your proof of citizenship, you had to fill out one of those federal W-4 forms, right?

Lesson 1: The money you earn over your lifetime isn't really all yours. The government always gets its share. Your pay stub will show you how much is taken out in federal taxes, unemployment insurance, and Social Security. Try to remember that the money deducted from your and everybody else's paycheck is what makes our government work. There may come a time when you will be glad unemployment insurance is there for you, and that Social Security is there for your parents. Additionally, your local governments may also deduct some money to help run your state or city.

If you live at home, you might be contributing something to household expenses on a monthly basis. As a newly minted, bona fide, grown-up wage earner, it is appropriate to contribute to family expenses if you wish to have a say in things that affect your home life. The more open you and your family are in the

nning about what is expected of you, the fewer misunder-
standings will occur later on. If you aren't asked to make a financial contribution to the family budget, you can figure out other
ways to contribute to family life.

Leana's mother felt that she should save as much as possible for
college. But Leana did contribute her time. "I pitched in with
household chores," she says. "And I spent a lot of time with my
younger half-brother and half-sister."

Aaron Seymour decided that saving money by living at home
was more important than living independently while he was with
the Conservation Corps in Pittsfield, Massachusetts. "AmeriCorps
paid minimum wage for a 30-hour week," he says, even though he
became a supervisor of a crew of eleven people his second year. He
did contribute to the family food budget but was still able to bank
a portion of his pay regularly.

Doug also lived at home, rent-free, for three months until he'd
saved some money. He loves to cook and did a major share of the
cooking for his family. Then he and a friend decided to share an
apartment. "But," he says, "rent was more than we could afford,
even with two salaries. We found a suitable place with three bed-
rooms and advertised for a third housemate." In the beginning,
Doug found that most of his paycheck went toward apartment
expenses.

Nate Kipp was able to save several thousand dollars over the
two years he worked with Habitat for Humanity through
AmeriCorps. He was very focused on what he wanted from his
working experience. "I was able to save a lot of money," says Nate,
"because I know how to live cheaply. The first year I was with
Habitat in Florida, I lived in a work camp. This year I'm at a
Habitat site in Cleveland, and I'm living in a Catholic Worker
community, which is low cost. I am not a Catholic, but this is a
very good situation. A few others of us live in this community. We
pay minimal rent, and we get our food. People take turns cooking.

We live with a total of 15 people. This can be difficult at times, but we manage to talk our differences out."

Sooner or later you will move out on your own. Before you do, think carefully about your goals for stopping out. Being financially independent is a laudable goal, but renting an apartment and choosing housemates can be a minefield, especially the first few times. Here are some suggestions from those with battle scars.

HOW TO RENT AN APARTMENT AND CHOOSE HOUSEMATES

1. Read your lease carefully before signing it. Better yet, take it home and have a parent or other adult read it over with you.

2. Know what you are getting: Can you add housemates? Will you have to pay for utilities? (If you live in a cold climate, winter heating bills can eat up your entire paycheck. The same is true if you are in a very hot climate and run the air conditioner day and night.) Are pets allowed? If you don't agree with certain clauses, discuss them with your landlord before you sign to see if he or she will delete them. Make sure the deletions are on both copies of the lease.

3. Don't sign a lease unless all of your housemates do so. You may be held responsible for the entire month's rent if your housemates fail to pay, so choose carefully!

4. Understand the terms of your security deposit—usually a portion of a month's rent which is to be refunded if you haven't done any damage to the place. If you notice holes in the walls, cracked or broken countertops, or marks on the floor, write it all down on a piece of paper and date it before you move in. Give one copy to your landlord and keep one along with your lease. When your lease is up, if there is no additional damage, you should get your security deposit back—with interest. If you or your housemates have put holes in the walls, ripped up the carpeting, or

otherwise damaged the apartment, you will be charged for repairs. All too often those repairs take up your entire deposit, so treat your apartment with respect.

5. Try to sign as short a lease as possible, or better yet, none at all. Be sure that if you have to leave before your lease is up, you can sublet your part of the apartment.

6. Best friends don't always make the best housemates. This comment was made by several people.

7. To avoid arguments over phone bills, don't install a phone. Each housemate can use his or her own cell phone. Make sure you have everyone's home address, so that if one person skips out without paying a utility or rent bill, you've got a place to contact him or her—or the person's parents.

8. Make it a rule not to lend money to any housemates, no matter how well you know them. You may wind up losing both a friend and your money. The same thing applies to you: Don't borrow money from your housemates.

9. Take the time to meet with all your housemates and discuss ground rules. Especially important is determining when bills are to be paid. Even if your housemates are late with their rent, phone, or utility bills, be sure to send in your share on time.

10. Set up strict guidelines regarding overnight visitors. If you don't do this in the beginning, you may find that you've acquired a nonpaying permanent guest who eats all your food, uses your shampoo, burns out your hair dryer, is always in your way, and is probably a slob.

11. Make sure that you and your housemates are in agreement on who is responsible for cleaning up common areas—kitchen, living room, and bathroom.

12. Be sure everyone understands rules of privacy and keeps out of your room and other personal space.

13. Keep valuables locked up.

14. Take out renter's insurance. It is generally inexpensive and could save you a great deal of money if your apartment is broken into or there is fire. NOTE: Few young people take this particular piece of advice until after something important, such as a bicycle, is stolen.

A WORD ABOUT USING CREDIT CARDS

Almost anyone can get a credit card these days—even if you don't earn much money. If you are a student when you apply for a credit card, you will have offers from virtually every credit card company in America. Credit card companies love to have you owe them money. In fact, the more you owe, the more credit card companies will want your business. And why not? After all, they make upwards of 18 to 20 percent a year on your unpaid balance. Of course, having a credit card can make a person feel very grown up. Who doesn't like to go out to a restaurant with a girlfriend or boyfriend, order a fine meal, pick up the check, and pay for it with a credit card? After all, hasn't the credit card company given you thousands of dollars of credit?

Just remember that as the owner of that card, YOU are responsible for paying off all the charges you run up, plus interest. So while it's tempting to run around charging all kinds of goodies on that card, there is always a day of reckoning. Sure, when you receive the monthly bill, you are given a minimum amount that you have to pay—1/36 of the total bill. If you don't make a substantial payment each month and keep running up bills, you will soon find yourself deep in credit card debt. Joe King, credit counselor at the Cornell Finger Lakes Credit Union in Ithaca, New York, estimates that one in four Americans winds up in serious credit card debt. Don't let it happen to you. The pattern of spending that you develop while you are young could trip you up later on in life. So while credit cards are a fact of life, and are useful, you need to be very cautious when using them.

Joe King is the person many people who get in over their heads in credit card debt come to for help. This is his advice:

1. Be discriminating when you are deciding which credit card offers to accept.

2. The first thing to look for is the federal disclosure information on the back of the offer. Yes, it is usually in small print, but read that small print carefully. (This information is required by law.) Try to avoid credit cards that have an annual fee. Don't accept a card that has a two-cycle balancing method for computing your average daily interest. In a two-tier system you are charged not only the interest on last month's unpaid balance, but also on your new purchases as well. In effect, you are being charged for two months at once. So while the interest rate may appear to be only 4.9 percent, you are really paying much more. The most common payment plan is simply the average daily balance—which is computed on a 30-day cycle. Also, the disclosure box carries the "teaser" offer at a very low interest rate. Be sure to see what the rate will change to after six months. Look for grace periods, normally 25 days.

3. Keep your credit limit low as long as you are a low wage earner or a student.

4. Establish a savings account before you apply for a credit card. You can use that account as collateral when applying for a card.

5. As a new credit card applicant, you may have to get a parent or other relative to cosign for your card. But if you get behind on your payments, it reflects on the cosigner as well. You don't want to be responsible for another person getting a bad credit rating because of your problem.

6. The way to establish a good credit rating is to make a payment on your account monthly and make it on time.

7. You can take a cash advance by using your credit card, but remember that the interest on a cash advance starts immediately, unlike the grace period when you purchase goods. And there may be a separate fee for a cash advance.

8. Before you make a purchase with your credit card, ask yourself if you NEED it or if you WANT it. Also, is this item a good value in terms of how often you will use it? If you don't NEED the item, but WANT it, try SAVING for it.

9. When you receive your monthly bill, check each and every item. If you see an error, call the toll-free number on the back of your card and tell them about the error. Be sure to follow up with any more information you have.

10. Don't let anyone borrow your card—ever.

11. Don't give your credit card number out over the phone unless it is to a very reputable company.

12. Be sure to make a monthly budget. The five most important areas of expenses to pay first are: housing, utilities, food, transportation, and yourself. Make saving a priority.

13. If you find yourself with too much credit card debt, call the credit card company and tell them you cannot meet the payments. Try to negotiate a lower monthly fee—and cut up your card until you get caught up.

14. If you still can't get straightened out, find a reputable credit counselor and get help.

PUTTING MONEY ASIDE

Unless you've grossly miscalculated, you will have some money left from each paycheck. Regardless of what your plans are for that money, you will probably want to open a savings account and perhaps a checking account.

If you are under 18, you may be surprised to learn that while all banks will be happy to let you put money into a savings account, not all of them will let you open a checking account. Said one bank manager, "Checking accounts can be a liability. Most young people don't know the basics of balancing a checkbook." Still, if you have a job, act like a serious person, and can demonstrate your need for a checking account, you can usually find a bank that will accommodate you. Another way to do this is to open a joint checking account with an older family member who won't use it, such as your mom or dad. Also, try to get yourself a line of credit, so that in case you do overdraw your account, you won't bounce a check. But remember that you have to write the bank a check for the overdraft or you get charged interest.

TIPS ON BANKING

1. Many banks require that you keep a minimum balance in checking and savings accounts, so wait until you have several hundred dollars before you make that initial deposit. In fact, some banks actually deduct money from your savings account if you go below their minimum balance! It's a good idea to shop around for the best deal. Many people report that credit unions are the most user-friendly, although not always in the best locations or with the best hours.

2. If you have a steady job, you may be able to arrange for a direct-deposit checking account, with your employer sending your paycheck directly to your bank.

3. Your ATM card frequently doubles as a debit card. This is convenient when shopping because you won't have to write a check. But it is not a real charge card. The money is taken directly out of your account, so when you use the card, be sure to enter the transaction in your check register. Do not ever let this card out of your possession, and don't let anyone else use it.

4. If you lose your card, report it to a bank official immediately.

5. Learn how to balance your checkbook and reconcile it with your bank statement each and every month. Remember, both you and the bank can make mistakes. If you have a problem, see a bank official immediately.

6. Make it a policy to put even a small amount of your paycheck in a savings account every payday. "Even when I was working just part time," says Dan Wallner, "I decided I'd never miss $25 a month, so that's how I started my savings account."

> **"I decided I'd never miss $25 a month, so that's how I started my savings account."**

KEEPING TRACK OF YOUR MONEY

If you don't make some sort of a budget, your money will be gone in a minute. The easy part is making the budget. The difficult part is sticking to it. So before you rush to move away from home, decide how you will spend your paycheck.

Housing

How much you pay for housing will vary from place to place. But even in large, expensive cities, you can find reasonable rents if you are willing to share your living space. Again, it depends upon your goals. Nate didn't think living in an apartment was important, so he was willing to explore alternative living arrangements while working for AmeriCorps.

Ryan Everhart, another AmeriCorps worker who served on a low-income housing project in Raleigh, North Carolina, found living on such a limited budget—$660 a month—too restrictive. In addition to the 50 hours a week he put in with

AmeriCorps, he waited tables for ten hours a week at a local college eatery. This also gave him a chance to meet people his own age.

One way to cut housing costs is to share an apartment or a house with several people. Check your local paper under listings such as "Housemate Wanted."

Food

This expense varies according to place, season, appetite, and how many times you get invited out to a free dinner. Two hundred dollars a month is probably a modest amount and doesn't take into account snacks, lunches at work, an occasional dinner out, or that inevitable late-night pizza. Paying for all of your own meals is a lot different from when you lived and ate at home.

> **"Paying for all of your own meals is a lot different from when you lived and ate at home."**

Tip: Buy a good basic cookbook and learn to make things from scratch. Make enough for leftovers. Doug says, "I used to buy a whole chicken and roast it. I'd put half in the freezer. That way I'd have a couple of meals during the week." Also, get your parents' best recipes for basic stuff like spaghetti with meatballs and macaroni and cheese. Keep staples like big jars of peanut butter and jelly on hand.

Tip: Bring lunch and snacks to work from home. Expensive lunches out can totally ruin your budget. "One of the good things about working in food service is that you get at least one meal free," says Matt.

Transportation

Is your job within walking distance of your home? Can you use a bike to get around town? Is public transportation readily available? Travel to and from work can be expensive, so be sure to figure it into your budget.

Recreation

Will you be able to afford a movie once or twice a month? Do you have to pay for cable TV? Do you or one of your housemates have a VCR or DVD player so you can rent movies and share the cost? Are there plays and concerts you want to go to? Once you know how much (or how little) you can budget each month for recreation, you may be very happy to just get together with a couple of friends, or invite them over to your place. (Have them bring the snacks.)

Use weekends to get together with friends to bike, hike, or backpack. Share transportation costs when traveling by car.

Personal items

When you lived at home, many personal items were provided for you. Now you are responsible for little things that add up to a lot

Other things you might consider . . .

➤ Membership at a local "Y" or health club. You might put this on your wish list of birthday or holiday presents.

➤ Discount tickets to plays.

➤ Find out if you can usher at special sporting events or concerts in exchange for a free ticket.

➤ Keep a wish list handy to give out to family and friends who may be generous at gift-giving times.

more money than you ever thought—toothbrushes, laundry soap, and toilet paper, for example—and bigger items such as that bargain sweater you spotted in the department store. You will also have to keep track of birthdays and other gift-giving occasions for friends and relatives. You are responsible for phone bills, too. You can probably count on most of the clothes already hanging in your closet, but eventually you will need to replace a number of basic items. All of these things need to be factored into your budget. Many of those who spend a year or two out in the working world learn to frequent thrift shops for great bargains. Says Doug, "Learning to live on a budget is an important part of growing up and becoming independent."

Health insurance

This is a major problem for young people. Most entry-level jobs and jobs in small businesses won't have any sort of health insurance for young workers. Your best bet is to see if you can stay on your parents' health plans until you become a student again. Most health insurance plans have some sort of a COBRA (Consolidated Omnibus Budget Reconciliation Act) plan that allows a parent to maintain a child who reaches the age of 18 (and is not in college) on their medical plan for a year or so for a separate monthly fee.

> ## "Learning to live on a budget is an important part of growing up."

Final thoughts: You need to be aware of items that are one-time costs and those that are ongoing. If the electric company requires a deposit before they will connect you, keep all receipts, and get your deposit refunded. Sometimes, if your parents have lived in your community for many years, the utility companies will waive the fees.

Checklist for Making a Monthly Budget

Unless you are a person who really loves little boxes and lots of numbers, making a monthly budget can be a bore. It is a good idea to keep your consumer desires to a minimum. Don't get sucked into buying things on credit. You've got plenty of time to develop those expensive tastes—save them for when you have money to indulge yourself. Here are the major things to keep on top of and review every two or three months:

➤ Your monthly income after taxes and the dates you get paid

➤ Date the rent is due

➤ Date the gas and electric bills are due

➤ Last day to pay the phone bill

➤ Monthly cable bill

➤ Weekly food costs

➤ Adding to your wardrobe

➤ Adding to your CD or book collection

➤ Necessary items to keep your living space in order

➤ Special events that require money

➤ Unexpected expenses

➤ Savings

Keep your checklist in a prominent place—taped to the wall above your desk, on the refrigerator, or next to your calendar. Keep close track of your expenses so you know where your money is going.

And don't forget that savings account. If you find your monthly expenses exceed your income, you may need to rethink plans for living away from home, look for a better-paying job, or take a second job.

Becoming an independent person is exciting. You won't have anyone looking over your shoulder, telling you how to manage your time when you are not working. But remember that handling your money responsibly is a major component of independence.

TIME ON YOUR HANDS AND NOT MUCH MONEY

What do people do when they're not sleeping, working, or eating? When you were a student, finding things to do with your leisure time wasn't difficult. If you weren't studying, you were hanging out with friends, partying, or getting involved in sports or other school activities. In fact, there were probably so many things to do, you never had to think about free time: There wasn't any.

Now that you are a working person, there is no one to tell you what to do. You don't have any homework. You can come home from your job, check out the refrigerator, turn on the TV, and watch it for as long as you want. If you do this every day, you will, as Doug notes, "becomes totally lethargic. You'll lose sight of why you really wanted to take time out."

One problem is that you no longer have a ready-made community of like-minded people to do things with. You don't have a lot of bucks to spend on entertainment, and most of all, you will not feel as if you're ready to join into all of those sober, adult activities your parents do. So what kinds of things are out there for you? What is it that the young working person does with his or her time?

Doug says, "At first I watched lots of TV. After a while I began to feel awful. My mind felt like it was turning to mush. So I made sure to buy a newspaper every single day. Not only did it keep me in touch with what was going on in the world, but the local paper kept me abreast of day-to-day events in my hometown. And I discovered there were many things going on that were free."

As it turned out, just reading the newspaper wasn't enough intellectual stimulation for Doug. (Most newspapers are written for the reading level of a sixth grader.) "I began to realize that I really didn't know very much about world events, so I'd follow some aspect of current events in the paper for a while, and then I'd call up my high school social studies teacher and ask her to recommend some books for me to read." Eventually, Doug got so interested in American politics that he audited a course at his local college.

Auditing college classes and other ways to learn

Many colleges and universities will allow you to audit courses for very little money if the professor agrees to let you sit in. Of course, you won't get the full benefit of your professor's teaching, since there are restrictions on what an auditor can and cannot do. Usually, but not always, papers you write won't receive the teacher's written criticism. You may take the tests but not receive a grade, and since you haven't paid the full tuition, you won't receive credit. Since there is no pressure to work for a grade, you are free to set your own limits on how much you wish to learn. You will really be in charge of your own education. Or you can register as an "extramural" student, pay full tuition for a course, and work for college credit that you may be able to transfer to the college of your choice at a later date.

Reading or attending classes may not be all you can do with free time. Go back and check out that plan you made for use of leisure time.

Leana decided to expand her interest in Japanese culture. But since she worked with books all day long, she joined a martial arts class in karate. "The day I actually broke a board with my bare hand was so exciting," she says. "I learned so much about how to

> ## "The day I actually broke a board with my bare hand was so exciting. I never knew what it was like to feel so strong."

control my own body. I never knew what it was like to feel so strong."

There is an awful lot of great stuff out there after working hours, if you are willing to make the effort. The most difficult part of sampling new activities is that often you won't have friends to go with you. "That's the advantage of signing up for a class," says Margie Ainslee, a young woman from Washington, D.C., who stopped out. "You don't have to go with anyone because you're doing it for yourself."

Taking courses on the Internet

Jonathan Finlay couldn't find classes he was interested in at the local colleges at a time that was convenient for him. Besides, he also hated sitting in a classroom. So he searched the Internet and found literally thousands of college and continuing education courses he could sign up for. "I'm interested in learning about computer programming and designing Web sites," he says. And he had no trouble finding dozens of courses that would fit the bill. "Some courses cost as little as $5 a month, while others will run $1,200 or more a semester. Of course the very inexpensive courses don't give you very much in the way of help. They simply publish new exercises and give you very little feedback." What Jon likes is that the more serious courses offer the opportunity for the student to interact with the professor both by e-mail and by phone. "And the chat rooms give you an opportunity to actively communicate with other people who are taking the course." That, coupled with the fact that you can log on to the course any time, makes taking courses online a very attractive alternative to a person who may not be able to get to a college campus. "I can do this on my own time," he says, "although most online courses give you a time limit in which you must finish the course. Online courses attract people who really want to learn—otherwise you won't keep up with the work." And, as with courses offered at colleges and universities, there is a grace period where if you decide the course isn't what you really wanted, most, if not all, of your tuition will be refunded.

MAKE THE MOST OF YOUR LEISURE TIME

1. "Keep your mind active. Make yourself read and debate the issues. If you aren't going to do that, you'll have trouble when you get into college."—Susan P. Staggers, former director of admissions, Mount Holyoke College

2. "A lot of what you do with your time depends upon where you are located. If you are in an urban setting, there are many cultural events available. On the other hand, you can also learn a lot if you're working in the Forest Service out in Idaho. The main thing I'd say is just don't stop reading. Reading is the whole process of communication. Keep in touch with the world." —Richard Pierson, former dean of admissions, Clark University

3. "I took a course in teaching reading to illiterate adults and then volunteered two evenings a week. It was the most rewarding thing I'd ever done."—Dick Lewis, Minnea

4. "I had a hard time getting a job in a ne ished job hunting each day, I went down to t paign headquarters, licked envelopes, and d congressman's re-election campaign. I even kids to get out some important mailings. I w

Was It Worth It?

"My work experience made me ready to try different kinds of things. I never thought I'd enjoy working in an office. But I liked dealing with customers."—Leana Horowitz

"I became so much more independent. I was not as intimidated by new situations. When I got to college, I had less trouble adjusting than did many of my classmates. And I had a lot more of an appreciation for school."—Rachel Reinitz

"In the long run, stopping out didn't make things better, but I learned not to worry so much."—Margie Ainslee

"At the time I stopped out, I found that work was more fulfilling than school. I couldn't figure out what I would study, so I thought school would be a waste. Working and living on my own was the best thing I could have done."—Chuck Bury

"College is a safe place. The real world is all about getting your next meal. My experience during the two years I stopped out taught me that I can get even a menial job and be satisfied. My friends who were students think school is hard. They see that when you're working, you have money. Well, I can tell you, it was hard to get."—Doug Leonard

"I loved working for a veterinarian, but I wasn't going to become a vet just by working for one. I needed to learn more. The jobs I had were all dead-end—so I decided to come back home and finish my bachelor's degree."
—Nora Schmidt

work I did, and it felt good to be doing a necessary task. One of the things I really treasure is a personal thank-you letter from my congressman after he was re-elected."—Gloria Simon, Worcester, MA

5. "Every weekend in good weather, I'd get together with other bicyclists, and we'd ride around the countryside. Sometimes we'd do 75 to 100 miles in one day. It was a great way to meet people and keep in shape."—Karen Levine, Sandy Hook, NJ

6. "I trained to become a 'techie' at my local radio station—and decided I loved radio enough to major in communications when I finally went off to college."—Doug Leonard, Northhampton, MA

7. "I got really involved in the Big Sister program in my community. And now that I'm in college, I still write to my little sister. I'm somebody she looks up to."—Lisa Martin, Baltimore, MD

WHERE ARE THEY NOW?

Many of the people I interviewed for this book have kept in touch with me. Several went to school after stopping out for a year. Others took a much longer time to get themselves into college.

Philip Bereaud spent more than five years traveling all over the United States, studying with Native Americans, working in Hawaii, and playing guitar and other musical instruments in a variety of bands. He finished a degree in music and composition at the Berklee College of Music in Boston and currently teaches music to preschool kids.

Sue Schwartz returned from her five months in Nepal and had a difficult time readjusting to life back in the United States. She is now a sophomore at Ithaca College and has finally realized her dream to go to Zimbabwe. She has been working all summer in one of the local eateries and saving her money. She will do a year with the School for International Studies, where she will learn about international development. "One thing I learned in Nepal is that you can't go into a community and say, 'OK, this is what you need, you could use a water tap'—and five years later, people come back and see that the water tap isn't working. They say, 'Why didn't you take care of that tap?' And the community leaders say, 'Well, you're the one who built it, why don't you do it?' People have to want development. It has to come from the people."

Doug Leonard majored in communications at the University of North Carolina, Greensboro. He did some radio and television work and signed on with Teach for America for two years. He now is a certified middle school teacher in Baltimore, Maryland, where he teaches science and computers.

Matt Thomas took business courses at Tompkins Cortland Community College and then transferred to the Hotel School at Cornell University.

Leana Horowitz graduated from Harvard University and then enrolled in the midwifery program at the Yale School of Nursing. She is now a midwife in Chicago, Illinois.

Nate Kipp went back to college. "I've had two years to grow up," he says. "I like construction, but I want to focus on my education." He graduated with a degree in mechanical engineering.

Sara Finegan apparently has satisfied her craving for travel and looks forward to graduating from Friends World Project. Her studies have taken her to London, Poland, and Germany, where she studied the history of World War II and the Cold War. She also studied Italian, Spanish, and German. The following year she enrolled in a comparative religions program and spent time living and studying in Taiwan, Thailand, and India. She found that different cultures have different concepts of privacy and "personal space." In India, she says, "I had to learn a whole new way of thinking about relationships with friends, and what this means, and what it means to be an American. It was really a humbling experience."

So it worked out for me. It wasn't the job I was looking for, but it was a job."

That summer, Anna basically did whatever was asked of her. Since the press was moving to new offices, Anna was "packing things up. It wasn't anything great, but I loved it. I was also stocking the bookshelves and seeing that letters were sent out."

The following summer, when Anna had finished her senior year, she came back to Dalkey as a paid intern. "I kind of knew I would get it, and it was so nice, because they had gotten to meet me. There was one other intern working with me that year. We still had to do the usual things, such as stocking shelves and stuff like that.

"But," Anna says, "we also started to read some books. I read two novels that year, and I was looking for mistakes and inconsistencies and things like that." In addition to printing new books, the publisher also reprints interesting out-of-print books. So Anna's task was to proofread the old version of the book. "If we were going to reprint it, we had to make sure there weren't any mistakes." One proved to be a real challenge. "It was modern fiction, and it didn't have punctuation, and it was difficult for me to get through it."

But after she finished, the book went to the marketing director, who also read it through. Anna got to see how the entire process worked, and she was pleased when the marketing department and the editor took her notes into consideration. "Not only was I working on the book side of things, but I also did jobs for the marketing director, I did sales, and I worked with the designer."

What made the internship different from a job was that each day Anna did something different. "Some days I even worked on contracts."

At the end of that summer, Anna headed off to the University of Illinois in Urbana-Champaign. When she came home over winter vacation, she and her co-intern were asked back as an extension of their internships. "So I was employed for a month over Christmas, when I normally would have just been sitting around." And, at the end of her freshman year, she returned to Dalkey as an assistant. "I'm doing some of the same things I did the first summer, but I've also learned some new things."

Anna's experience with the Dalkey Archive Press has shown her that there are many opportunities for an English major like herself who loves to read and write. And her experience was very satisfying. "It's a wonderful place to work. It's very laid back. This is a hands-on experience, and it's really a welcoming place."

Anna's internship program was funded by the Illinois Arts Council. She worked 20 hours per week and was paid $8.50 per hour.

Dalkey Archive Press
ISU Campus Box 8905
Normal, IL 61709-8905
(309) 438-7555
aweaser@dalkeyarchive.com

Anna's internship fits the description of what a good internship should be. According to Jane G. Kendall, former director of the National Society for Internships and Experiential Education, there are three things that make an internship different from serving as a volunteer or working at an entry-level job.

First, there is a partnership between the sponsor and the intern. The sponsor agrees to make sure the intern explores a wide range of tasks in a particular business or agency.

Second, there is a learning agenda for the intern. The intern (that's you) is expected to ask lots of questions, work hard, and come away from the experience with an understanding of a particular subject area, organization, or agency.

Finally, the intern goes through a continuous process of reflection, so that he or she can begin to understand both theory and actual practice during and after the experience. If you complete the internship as part of a school assignment, you will be asked to submit a written report about your experience. This may include a critique of your particular organization. Or your sponsor may ask you to write a report to help make the next intern's experience better—or at least as good as yours. If you are doing this internship as part of a college experience, you may be asked to present your project to other professionals, fellow interns, or your professor.

A good internship is this mix of intentional learning and periodic reflection.

ONE SIZE DOES NOT FIT ALL

Internships come in all sizes.

➤ An internship may be part-time or full-time.

➤ An internship may be as short as one month or as long as two years.

➤ An internship may be paid or unpaid, or involve a fee.

➤ An internship may be sponsored through an educational institution, or arranged independently by the intern herself or a host organization.

➤ An internship may or may not provide an intern with high school or college credit.

➤ An internship may have a variety of goals—academic, ethical, career building, and/or personal and social development.

What distinguishes an internship from a job or a volunteer experience is that the intern is encouraged to do some or all of the following:

➤ Acquire, apply, integrate, and evaluate a body of knowledge or the methodology of an academic discipline.

➤ Understand different cultures and environments.

➤ Acquire generic academic skills, e.g., identification of a problem, analysis, and synthesis.

➤ Develop and use an ethical perspective in complex situations.

➤ Develop knowledge and skills specific to a particular occupation, profession, or organizational setting.

➤ Acquire general skills for effective adult life, e.g., oral communication, interpersonal interaction, coping with ambiguity, working in groups, setting goals, managing time—precisely the skills that will be important to you when you are out in the working world.

➤ Explore career options and gain documented work experience in a field that requires college-level knowledge and skills.

FINDING THE RIGHT INTERNSHIP

So, how do you actually find the internship that's right for you? And how do you make sure you get the most out of the experience?

It helps to have something specific in mind, so begin by asking yourself some questions:

➤ What are my interests? Do I want to work with my hands? Do I want to explore a scientific field? Learn about a particular business? Explore a career in television or radio?

➤ Where would I like to do this? In my hometown? In another part of the country? In another country?

➤ Do I want to be with other people my own age? Or doesn't it matter, so long as I'm learning something interesting?

You can begin by checking in with your guidance or career counselors at school. They often get a lot of brochures from organizations offering internships, and they don't always have the time to sort through them. You might also ask a favorite teacher whose subject you especially like whether he or she knows of any opportunities for a summer internship. Or try utilizing the Internet by searching for "internships for high school students." You will find some excellent Web sites with plenty of information. Pick a few and check them out. Do remember that many internships are very competitive and have specific deadlines. Others are less so and have rolling admissions. Narrow the field down to one or two, three at most, and fill out the applications.

But even before you begin your research, you need to be aware that while some internships will carry a stipend, others do not. And, in fact, some internships require that you (or your family) pay a hefty fee. Don't be discouraged if the amount of money required seems out of reach. In many cases, partial or whole scholarships are available. If you find something that seems unaffordable, don't be afraid to ask about scholarship or sponsorship possibilities. Or, if you apply far enough ahead of time, you can probably earn some of the money you will need. Keep in mind that a successful internship can help you reap great rewards down the road.

It pays to be careful in choosing your internship

How can you be certain that the internship you've chosen is going to be legitimate? How do you know if it's right for you? Sometimes even well-established programs turn out not to be what you bargained for.

This happened to Dara Silverman. During her sophomore year at Bard College, she went to the career and development center to look over the internship possibilities. When she came upon an organization billed as a clearinghouse on marital and date rape, she became very excited.

"I knew I wanted to do an internship that was involved in women's issues. I'd been involved with the [local] rape crisis center when I was in high school. So it was natural for me to want to expand my education in this area. I figured it would lead me into crisis counseling."

Dara had read about this particular organization in "a bunch of different books." So she phoned the director at her home in California, and the woman seemed eager to have Dara come out there. Even though she would have to pay her own way, make her own living arrangements, and support herself, Dara was eager to go. "But when I got there, it was a little more than I'd bargained for."

The organization had no offices. The entire operation was in the director's home. "And she had allergies, so everyone had to change their clothes when they got there and cover their hair and heads with *shmattes* [rags]. And she had this cast-off clothing—pink pants suits that she'd make people put on. I never had such an experience. It was so disorganized. There were people everywhere. She had dozens of interns coming from all over the country."

Not surprisingly, many of the interns left right away. But Dara decided that since she'd come clear across the continent, she might as well stay a while.

Dara wound up organizing the files on a very high-profile rape case. "But there really wasn't any space for me to do this, so I'd sit on the floor next to a sliding glass door, which didn't shut all the way. And it was raining almost the entire month. There was a vent on the other side of the room that was blowing up hot air. So I was cold on one side and hot on the other."

Despite the inconveniences, Dara completed the task and ended up writing two papers on the trial. "And I did get to meet interns from almost every part of the country—Florida, Utah, New York State." They had all come for many of the same reasons as Dara. The director had a national reputation because, Dara said, "She was very instrumental in getting marital rape laws on the books in the '70s and '80s. She has good credentials. But she has a million different things going on at once, and her home isn't a well-constructed place to work in."

How could Dara have avoided making this mistake? She admitted that if she had contacted other organizations that did anti-rape work, she might have discovered the problem before she flew to California. "And," she says, "it would have been useful to talk to other interns. When I returned to Bard, people came up to me and said, 'Oh, I heard that you did an internship there.' And I said, 'Well, if you don't mind working in the midst of chaos, then you can do it. But if you want an organized experience, don't go there.'"

Some words to make you wiser

1. Don't get carried away by the reputation of the agency or organization. Before you agree to become an intern, get a written description of the work you will be expected to do.

2. If you are going to be traveling a great distance, check with other similar organizations in the same city or area to find out what they think about the one you've chosen.

3. Talk to at least two people who have done the internship recently. If you get conflicting reports, ask another person.

4. If you do wind up in a difficult situation, you have choices. You can quit and try to find another situation in the same area, or you can quit and go back home. Or you can, as Dara did, find something interesting to focus on and make the experience work for you.

Finding an internship at home

Jonathan Kuhl from Fayetteville, New York, always had an interest in politics. So when Senator Charles Schumer opened an office in nearby Syracuse, Jonathan contacted Jill Harvey, the senator's administrative aide, and applied for a summer internship. Jonathan was 15 at the time and a rising high school sophomore. Even though Ms. Harvey wasn't quite certain how a high school student would work out, she was willing to give him a chance.

"At first," says Jonathan, "I was just answering the phones. People would call in just to voice an opinion on various upcoming bills, or perhaps on some personal problem, and a lot of times a personal phone call from the senator's office was just enough to solve a problem."

The best part of the internship was that Ms. Harvey allowed Jonathan to do things that regular staff members did. "I was treated as a person working there alongside her." Jonathan was allowed to listen in on conference calls along with the full-time staff, for example. And when Senator Schumer came to Syracuse, Ms. Harvey would "bring me along and let me help out with the event. I had to make sure the press was there, made certain that so-and-so from the local television or radio station was there. And while the senator was speaking, I needed to know what the next event was, and if the senator needed something to eat, I'd go out and grab something for him."

Ms. Harvey was also very thoughtful. When she introduced Jonathan to Senator Schumer for the first time, she brought along a disposable camera and took their picture together.

Jonathan also had an opportunity to take charge of a project. There were two groups of veterans who wanted to bring a VA hospital to Syracuse, but each group had a special interest in a different site. While it was clear that the hospital would become a reality, it was important not to alienate either group. Jonathan's idea was to bring the leaders of both groups, along with a state assemblywoman, to a joint meeting in the senator's district office, with Ms. Harvey and himself moderating. "It wasn't a huge press event, but it was important that the two sides sat down to discuss the issue, and the meeting allowed them to see that one side wasn't out to 'get' the other." The meeting was "the highlight of that summer" for Jonathan. He was invited to intern for two more summers.

He is now a government major at Hamilton College. This past summer, while earning money working for the parks department, he also did an internship with the producer of the 11:00 news at an NBC affiliate in Syracuse, and he's now shadowing the news reporters to see how they go out and report stories. He also gets to write the 15–30 second spots the news anchor reads.

"While politics has always been my main interest," Jonathan says, "this gives me an opportunity to see how politics and the media merge."

To find out if your congressperson or senator has internship openings either in their Washington, D.C., offices or in their home districts, you can check out the Web sites of individual members of Congress. Although many of the openings are for college students, sometimes, like Jonathan, you can luck out and land a summer internship right at home.

What if you don't want to be in an office? What if you want to immerse yourself in something really different?

Well, Sara Bumgardner had no idea when she began a research project for her A.P. science class at her high school in Muncy, Pennsylvania, that she'd be invited to apply for an internship at the Jackson Laboratory in Bar Harbor, Maine. She couldn't work on any of her ideas for her high school project because of the limitations of the lab at school. But an aunt, who taught in Maine, suggested Sara contact Jon Geiger, director of education at the Jackson Labs, for suggestions on how to do her project. Not only did Jon give her suggestions as to where she could find information on her project, he later encouraged her to apply for a summer internship at the Jackson Labs.

"I was a little hesitant, because I was concerned about the time. I was still in high school and hadn't really ever been away from my family or friends. So going away for the entire summer by myself to something new was a little scary for me. But I decided it would be a good opportunity, so I applied. And when I was accepted, I got really excited, and then I really wanted to go." Her bout of homesickness when she arrived in Bar Harbor lasted exactly one day.

"It was such a great experience for me. The lab experience and the collaboration aspect, being able to talk intellectually with my mentor as a researcher, and to get feedback with ideas was great. In the beginning I had to struggle to understand what was going on. The first week I had to learn exactly what my project was." Sara was to do a protein analysis of ancrin.

In addition to the work, there was a social side to Sara's experience. There were 33 interns, a third of whom were high school students. The rest were college students, and they all lived together in a mansion that was right on the water. On weekends there was always something to do. "On weekends we'd go hiking and rock climbing and swimming. I definitely explored every aspect of the island while I was there. One Saturday, my friends and I spent nine hours and twenty minutes hiking every one of the peaks in Acadia National Park. And one weekend we did a quadrathalon—about 15 of us swam, hiked a trail, biked, and raced each other. It was really fun to see the competitiveness come out in everybody. I was pleased that I beat one of my friends, Brad, by a minute." Another time she and her friends biked 22 miles. And everyone, Sara said, was involved in Ultimate Frisbee.

"What I learned was that there is so much out there in terms of doing research. My mentor wanted me to get the lab experience, but she also wanted me to enjoy the social aspect. There are people here from all over the world, and we really meshed."

While Sara's career goal of becoming a veterinarian hasn't changed, she now sees that the door to research has been opened. She earned a stipend of $2,500 for her summer's work, which she will apply toward college.

Sara Bumgardner (front row, left), with other young scientist interns, takes time out from her work at the Jackson Labs to go kayaking on Moose River in Maine. (Sara Bumgardner)

The Jackson Laboratory
600 Main Street
Bar Harbor, ME 04609-6260
(summer program contact: Jon Geiger, director of education)
(207) 288-6000
training@jax.org
http://www.jax.org
Note: Deadline for applying is early January, and more than 300 people apply each year.

AN OPPORTUNITY TO EXPERIENCE A DIFFERENT CULTURE

Leah Fagan's semester on the island of Crete not only introduced her to a totally different living experience, it also included an internship that helped her to understand another culture. The moment she and the 13 other students arrived on the island, they were whisked away to the tiny village of Kolimbari, famous for its olives, citrus fruits, vegetables, and wine. There were large numbers of sheep and goats roaming the island. It was nothing like her suburban home in New Jersey. Her home for the next several months would be on a hilltop overlooking the Aegean Sea, in a compound with a courtyard, similar to the way families live on the island. The students and tutors all lived in the same buildings and shared in the work of keeping their living and working space neat and clean.

Within the first week, Leah had mastered enough Greek to be able to go into town, read the signs, and order a simple meal in a restaurant.

In addition to a rigorous academic program that included archaeology, Greek language, history, and creative writing, Leah and her classmates were assigned to work with individual families every morning. "The girls worked with the women, and the boys worked with the men. The women were all housewives. That's the culture. My routine was to take the family's two kids to school, and then I shadowed the mom. We'd cook two meals each day. We did laundry. We helped out in the shop [a grocery store owned by the husband]. During the olive harvest, the boy who was working in the shop and I, and the whole family, went to the olive grove and picked olives. If there were a special birthday party, we'd get invited. We became like members of the family."

All the internships became "a day in the life of . . ." Since no one in the family spoke English, Leah learned pretty quickly to communicate in Greek. After she completed her morning work, she returned to the compound where the students lived, ate and studied.

"The culture is very different from our own," says Leah. "It's almost as if it's a 'shame' culture. I mean, everybody is in everybody's business; everybody knows everything, and privacy doesn't exist. It's like, 'It takes a village to raise a child' sort of thing."

Her most memorable experience was in September. "It was grape-harvest season, and the local farmers know that there are 14 extra hands around town, so they hire us to harvest the grapes, along with the rest of the villagers.

"So we are harvesting grapes and we're having this feast, and it's just incredibly romantic and fantastic. We were doing this as a group—singing songs in the field, and then the villagers would feed us, and then we got to stomp the grapes! Literally, just like you see in one of the *I Love Lucy* reruns. It's just unbelievable. There is this little old lady who owns the farm, and she is feeding us candy, and we are dancing and then they feed us again." When the grape stompers stepped out of the tubs, "this little old lady would wash our feet," Leah says.

The semester-long experience, for Leah, was "a voyage of self-discovery, and you come back with so much self-awareness. We were learning about ourselves the entire time, through our tutors, through ourselves, and through the community."

Coming back home was difficult. "Here I have my own shower, and there's nobody to talk to while I'm taking a shower. In Crete we're all in everybody's business, and it was very weird being behind closed doors again."

Leah believes that the experience changed her. "I think I'm easier to live with now. I think I share my space and communicate a lot better with other people about what I might need. I think that dealing directly with people—living, sleeping, breathing with people 24/7—shakes your bubble."

When she began life as a college student at Middlebury College, she found that she received full credit for her "Ithaka" semester. "And," Leah says, "it wasn't expensive in terms of what I got out of it. It was less expensive than a semester at Middlebury College."

COMMUNAL LIFE AT SEA

Allison Novelly's 80 days at sea through Sea-mester proved to be a life-affirming adventure for her. Her voyage started in the British Virgin Islands. The shipmates and staff traveled to Nevis, Grenada, St. Vincent, St. Lucia, Martinique, St. Bart's, Antigua, and back to the British Virgin Islands.

"But this is not a cruise. It's an integrated approach," says Allison. "Students and staff work together, cleaning the boat, cooking the food, shopping for food. Each shipmate and each staff member had a different task daily. You can be the skipper one day, you can be the engineer, you can be the chef, the dishwasher—all different things, so everyone has the opportunity to learn all different jobs, and there's no separation between staff and shipmates. Everyone works together."

Not everything runs smoothly, nor is everything easy. Even though Allison had more sailing and scuba diving experience than many other shipmates, living 24/7 in close quarters requires a specific set of skills. "On a boat, there is only so much space. Each shipmate has a bunk, and on the catamarans there were cabins that a few people shared. But there's only so much space in which to get away from someone if you're mad at them. It forces you to really deal with issues and confront problems. I think that we learned a lot about how to deal with things in our own lives."

Besides learning about the sailing vessel's functions and becoming certified scuba divers, the students attend regularly scheduled classes. "What makes [the classes] so exciting is an enthusiastic and talented staff who encourage the students to believe in themselves, and what we come away with is, 'Wow! I did a lot of things I didn't know I was able to do.'" Allison says what was so exciting was that the classes were hands-on. In marine biology, "We went out and did lab projects on different islands." She worked with marine conservationists to create artificial reefs so that the coral plants will be able to regenerate.

By the end of the voyage, Allison felt she had the confidence to try new and different things. "You know, this is an issue many of us struggle with. And this confidence has carried over into other aspects of my life."

Greg Skinner found Sea-mester through the Internet. "When I read about it, I just said, 'I have to do this.'" He chose the 40-day "mini-mester" offered during the summer, and even made use of the college credit option by transferring the six credits in oceanography and basic seamanship to Rochester Institute of Technology, where he is currently a junior majoring in information technology. He loved everything about the program. "From the first day you are there, you are on this schooner with 13 other people, and you live together as a family. I experienced so much that it completely changed my idea of what I wanted to do

Allison Novelly and Torin Tofferi lean off the bowsprit of Ocean Star *on passage to the island of Saba.* (Allison Novelly)

with my life." His dream now is to get his captain's license and own his own boat. "There are no words to express what happens out there on a Sea-mester voyage. It's really magical. After that experience, when I flew home, I couldn't get Sea-mester out of my head." And when he was asked to come back to work on the Action Quest sailing program for high school kids, he was thrilled.

"But," Greg says, to be successful on a sailing voyage such as Sea-mester, "you have to have an open mind. If all you want to do is sunbathe, well, you probably won't do too well. You don't have to be a super swimmer, either, but you do have to know how to swim 200 meters and tread water for 10 minutes." The rest, you will learn from experts.

A SAMPLER OF INTERNSHIPS

Perhaps you'd like to explore a variety of internships over the course of a year or even a semester. Gloria Shepard wasn't sure what she wanted to do after she finished high school. She did know she wanted to get "away from Michigan and all the things I already knew."

Her guidance counselor suggested she check out an internship program in Worchester, Massachusetts, called Dynamy, Inc. Dynamy provides post–high school students with a yearlong series of internships at a huge number of businesses and nonprofit organizations. Students live four to an apartment in buildings owned by Dynamy, and before their internships begin, they all take part in a weeklong Outward Bound experience.

"My parents were really against this," Gloria said. "My mother thought I wouldn't ever go to college, and my father thought it was just a bad idea." But Gloria thought otherwise, and her application was so strong that she landed a full scholarship for the year. "I only had to pay for my travel," she said. Gloria had no trouble earning that money during the remainder of her senior year and summer after graduation.

Besides the internship experience, Dynamy also employs 40 student advisers who help the interns settle in, provide support, and give advice during the internships. Advisers help students sort out their college aspirations, if they decide that's the next step. If the interns wish to, they may attend class one evening a week along with their internships and earn up to 12 college credits through Clark University.

Gloria loved everything about her experience. The Outward Bound week had a powerful impact on her—both in acquiring the skill and confidence to scale a 50-foot wall and jump from a ledge onto a tree stump, but also in understanding the importance of teamwork. It even changed her idea of where she wanted to go to college and what she wanted to study. When she entered New College in Florida the following year, she decided to major in environmental studies.

She did three internships over the year, including one with a state senator who had offices in Worcester. The highlight of the internship was when she was called upon to organize a community-based daylong informational program. "I organized a program for representatives of 25 state agencies to meet with some of the senator's really poor constituents so they would know how to utilize these agencies. That meant I sent out letters to both the agencies providing services and the people who used them. I called people on the phone and went door-to-door to let constituents know we were seriously interested in their participation."

Remember Chris Batt from Chapter 1? He was feeling pretty much at loose ends after an unsuccessful year in college. But he had this notion that he wanted to work in television. When an academic counselor suggested Dynamy as a possibility, he decided to go for it, even though it meant starting during the spring semester. The Outward Bound spring offering turned out "to be cross-country skiing and dog sledding. I loved it," he said. "I'm an outdoors kind of guy."

Chris got his wish to work at the local TV station, where he did "everything. I went out on shoots, used the camera, and got to do online news." He also quickly decided that television was not for him. "I didn't want this as a career."

It was his second internship that helped Chris land an excellent job a year later. "I wanted to learn more about rowing. I'd been involved with crew and physical education all my life," he said. The internship at an engineering firm gave him hands-on experience, plus a lot of responsibility. The firm where Chris interned built and designed boats for racing. "I learned what it takes to build rowing boats, kayaks, even the oars. I learned more about rowing—every aspect of it."

Chris tried college again, but after another semester, he decided he was ready to start his career. "Now I'm a sales rep for a hydraulic company. And the engineering internship helped me enormously—especially in understanding how things work. I love what I'm doing now."

The kind of person who does well at Dynamy is someone who really wants to be involved in his or her own education and who is somewhat of a risk taker. Although some kids may have a hard time living on their own—they have to live on a budget, get up for work on time, and get along with their housemates—the rewards are worth it. Chris said, "When I lived at home I never worried about what I spent." He knew his parents would always pick up the bills. But at Dynamy, he actually "learned to live on a budget."

Dynamy recently expanded its program to the West Coast.

Dynamy Inc.
27 Sever Street
Worchester, MA 01609
(508) 755-2571
info-email@dynamy.org
http://www.dynamy.org/

A couple of important things stood out for people who chose to do an internship or an internship with a specific study program.

➤ As important as the internship was, equally important was the self-confidence gained by the individuals.

➤ None of the students whom I interviewed for this book looked upon the internship solely as something that would look good on a future résumé.

➤ People who did these internships had a great sense of adventure and a real thirst for knowledge.

➤ All had an open mind, even when things didn't work out.

➤ For those who went on adventure internships, community became an important aspect of the programs, and all of them offered courses in community building and conflict resolution. Heidi Stucker, who went on a yearlong expedition to the Pacific Northwest with the Audubon Expedition Institute says, "Having been an avoider, and [one] who kind of walks around conflict and stays away from it as much as possible, I became much more conscious of myself and made an effort to work with it, and to recognize that conflict happens. Now I have the skills to confront someone in a respectful way."

➤ Interns often become more conscious of how to live a far simpler life than the one they've been accustomed to. Greg Skinner says, "I learned that there is so much more out there besides what I was doing in college."

Heidi Stucker (left) with another student outside the Audubon Expedition Institute bus (Heidi Stucker)

➤ "We have a special group of friends now. In Greek it's called 'parrea'—we have e-mails going back and forth all the time. Some of my friends [from the Ithaka program] are out in L.A. and are going to be making a film together," reports Leah Fagan.

Chapter VI

How to Change the World During Your Summer Vacation

"THE WEIRDEST THING I EVER ATE," SAYS DAN ELSBERG, "WAS ARMADILLO. And the funny thing was that the armadillo was walking around the backyard that afternoon, when suddenly this guy pulls out his pistol and shoots the thing. And the next thing we knew, it wound up on the table. Cooked, of course."

That was during the summer after Dan's junior year in high school. He was in a tiny village in Paraguay with three other American high school students. They had joined up with a program called Amigos de las Americas—Friends of the Americas. Their mission was to spend eight weeks on an immunization project.

"My job was to give shots to children: measles, mumps, whooping cough, rubella, tetanus, and also I administered liquid polio vaccine." There were other tasks, as well. "We'd go into the school and give out toothbrushes and teach kids how to brush their teeth, give mini-lectures in the church or school, and leave information with the teachers on the importance of the immunizations."

Dan's living accommodations were something less than spartan, but they were more luxurious than all but three or four of the 200 families in the village of Encarnaca. Dan and the other male member of this intrepid quartet were housed in the home of the brother of the town doctor. The two girls lived at the new clinic. What set their lodgings apart was that both the house and clinic had glass windows, and the outdoor latrines were enclosed.

While most of the villagers appreciated the work Dan and the other kids were doing—indeed, Amigos goes only into communities that request its services—sometimes there were quarrels among the elders. In return for the services provided by Amigos, the town agrees to feed and house the students. "Some of the community people thought that my hosts were embezzling the food money. I never found out if this was true," said Dan. But it was decided that the students would eat at a local restaurant. And at the end of their stay, the restaurant owner complained that he hadn't been paid. "So it fell to us when we were dispensing the polio vaccine to ask the villagers if they had paid their share." This made Dan very uncomfortable. "That wasn't supposed to happen."

> "One father said, 'I had eleven kids and four of them died of measles. I am so glad that you are here.'"

But most of the experience was excellent. Even though some people were wary of the North American medicine, others would come up to Dan and say how much they appreciated their work. "One father said, 'I had eleven kids and four of them died of measles. I am so glad that you are here.'"

There were other rewards, including learning about another culture. Dan found the people in the village were "responsible for themselves and had a great sense of community. Their time is different from our time. What I saw in Latin America is that it is a great burden to feed four people. The hardest thing for me was coming back home. There was such culture shock. We have so much, and I would think, 'Why do I need it all? I love having my stereo and computer and video games, but I really don't need these.'" Fortunately, Amigos had prepared the volunteers for these feelings and had suggested ways to cope. A big plus was that Dan's Spanish improved so much that when he went to college a year later, he signed up for a Spanish literature course where the reading and discussions were all in Spanish. "There is no way I could have done that with just two years of high school Spanish."

Are you someone who thinks the world is pretty messed up, and there isn't much you can do about it? Well, you're partly right. There's a lot that needs to be done to make the world a better place.

The good news is, it isn't your fault. You never asked to be born into this world. To tell the truth, neither did anybody else. In fact, the world has always been somewhat of a mess.

The bad news is, this is the only world we have (as far as we know), and your generation is stuck with the job of figuring out how to make things better. Actually, every generation gets stuck with that task, and some do a better job than others. If you are one of the people who wants to create a better world, that is good news indeed. There are many ways you can do your part.

While it may seem far-fetched that an ordinary 18-year-old can make a contribution to saving the environment, right an injustice, create a better place for the homeless, or feed the hungry, there really are things a young person can do to make the world a little better. No, you don't have

> **"This is the only world we have, and your generation is stuck with the job of figuring out how to make things better."**

to become president of the United States, and you don't have to find a cure for AIDS or cancer. Nor do you have to be the one to plug the hole in the ozone layer. You can save those big-ticket items for another time—or leave it for your kid brother or sister.

You can, however, commit a block of time to community service in your hometown, your state, another part of the country, or a foreign country. You can do this for three or four weeks over the summer, or take six months or an entire year after you finish high school to help improve life in one corner of the world. (You'll find yearlong projects sprinkled throughout other chapters.)

The astonishing thing is that while you are doing something for someone else, the people you are working with are doing something positive for you. What you get back will be different for each of you.

Don't be put off by the cost of a program. According to Gideon Levenberg, longtime social activist and former project administrator in Guatemala with Guatemala Partners, "Many students who

Before You Take Time Out for Community Service, You Need to Figure Out:

➤ Do you prefer a community group, a religious organization, or a government (city, county, state, or federal) agency?

➤ How much time do you have to give to a project—a couple of weeks in the summer, an entire summer, a semester, or a year?

➤ Must you earn money, or can you participate in a project that requires a fee for travel and living expenses?

➤ Would you be more comfortable in a structured environment where your work is laid out for you each day, or are you a self-starter who can be comfortable figuring out things on your own?

do community service in Latin America have had extraordinary experiences volunteering with organizations that charge fees.

"Sometimes these programs cost the volunteer money. At first it sounds like a lot of money, especially if there is airfare involved. But that shouldn't put you off. You can save for it by working after school or during vacations. Also, many of the organizations will help you with fund-raising ideas, and sometimes there are partial scholarships. Think of it as an investment. You will get to learn a new language if you go to a foreign country. It is a new kind of living experience, and you will be making a contribution to the community. This kind of activity will also help you get into college or will help you get a job. Companies like to hire people who get involved in community service."

SUMMER PROGRAMS FAR AND NEAR

Evan Webster's experience with Amigos was quite different from Dan's. For one thing, because Evan lived in Boston, where there was an established chapter of Amigos, his training sessions were held every Tuesday for two and a half hours from November until the end of May. Evan estimated that 50 students gathered for these sessions, which were conducted by experienced volunteers from other Amigos programs. Dan, on the other hand, wasn't near an Amigos volunteer center, so he received a planning book and worked through it on his own. Once he knew what his assignment was, he met several times with his family physician and dentist to ask questions. Before he left for Paraguay, he joined other Amigos participants in Houston, where he learned to inoculate many dozens of oranges before he was allowed to try it out on human beings.

Evan's planning sessions included discussions about what it would be like living in another country, how to adjust, and what to expect when the volunteers arrived in that country. Also, he says, "We had some Spanish practice, and in addition, there was one weekend where we were supposed to speak Spanish for the whole weekend (but we cheated). We took part in various activities and became immersed in what we might expect."

Evan was excited when he learned he was going to his first choice country—Oaxaca, Mexico—for a six-week project. When he first arrived, he and the others assigned to this area were housed in a church, where they had four days of pre-assignment training. Evan and two girls wound up in a small village, about a four-hour drive from Oaxaca and 8,000 feet above sea level. At first it was a bit difficult adjusting to the thin air at such a high altitude, but by the time the first week ended, everyone had acclimated. They were assigned to stay in the local convent, which had some beds for guests. Except for the fact that they had to be back at the convent by 9 P.M. every night, that worked out just fine.

"We started working at the music school," says Evan. It was a boarding school where children from several villages lived, and for half their stay, the Amigos contingent ate their meals with the children. Evan and one of his partners taught English, while the third member of the trio taught piano. They also helped with non-medical tasks in the local clinic, which was staffed with doctors and nurses.

The main thing Evan's group accomplished was to set up and run a day camp for the village children from ages seven to 12. There were problems, but the three overcame them as they became more comfortable with the local population. "There were very few white people in the village, and certainly no Americans, and the language issue was a big problem. And also, the local government thought that the Amigos kids were experts in reforestation, and that we were professionals and that we'd have very good Spanish. And that wasn't the case. Nevertheless," Evan concludes, "the people really appreciated us a lot."

At the end of his stay, Evan felt he could have done more. "I thought there might have been towns that needed more help from us." And he wasn't certain that his contribution was "that great." He also thought that he benefited more than the villagers did. "It was a once-in-a-lifetime experience for me. My Spanish improved, and as a result of this experience, I became more interested in Spanish. I also became more aware of what people go through just to live, and how lucky I am to live in the United States."

Amigos de las Americas projects

Amigos de las Americas is privately funded and has been operating for 40 years. It carries out programs in Mexico, Costa Rica, Paraguay, Ecuador, the Dominican Republic, Honduras, Bolivia, and Brazil. The program cost is between $3,425 and $3,625. Students will also need pocket money and airfare to either Houston or Miami. Amigos provides volunteers with ideas for fund-raising. There are four-week, six-week, and eight-week projects. Students work in groups of two or three, or occasionally in larger groups. Volunteers are placed with youth leaders and field staff, all of whom are veterans of the program. Amigos looks for people who are either entering junior or senior year in high school or who have graduated. You will need a basic understanding of Spanish (or Portuguese for Brazil), which will definitely improve while you are in the program. At least two years of Spanish is required, and more is better.

Amigos de las Americas
5618 Star Lane
Houston, TX 77057
(800) 231-7796
info@amigoslink.org
http://www.amigoslink.org
Note: There is a $25 application fee.

An opportunity to do field research

Chris Golden used to watch all those nifty animal programs on TV when he was a kid. "And," he says, "Ever since I was little, I wanted to go to Madagascar. I was always interested in unique animals." In the summer after his sophomore year in high school he joined up with Earthwatch Institute, a private organization that supports environmental research throughout the world. And he got his wish. He was off to Madagascar for a two-week stint.

Chris worked with Luke Dollar, the principal investigator of the project. In the two weeks he was there, Chris worked on taking the census of a predator known as the fossa. "It's related to civets and mongooses. We would set up traps and take all kinds of measurements and paw prints and blood work. And we put radios on them so we could track them." Chris learned a lot about this rare and elusive animal. "It looks like a very low-slung puma, and

Golden and other volunteers with the elusive fossa in Madagascar.
olden)

there's an article in *International Wildlife* which said that kilo for kilo, the fossa is the most ferocious animal on earth. They are very scared of humans, and although there are a few reports of them attacking infants, none has been substantiated."

Chris worked with 11 other volunteers in Madagascar. "We had the largest age range they've ever had. I was 16, and the two oldest women were 69. They were the best friends I made, and I'm still in touch with them. I just had dinner with them last month. There was another 16-year-old, someone who was 18, and the project director was around 24. The others were in their 40s." The two oldest participants, Chris said, had been on 17 or 18 projects!

Chris's first experience was so successful that he signed up to go to a wildlife hippo sanctuary in Ghana the next summer. "It's called Wechiau. We were doing a species-wide wildlife and plant inventory so that it could gain status as a national park and become a tourist attraction that would raise money for the community as well as a safe haven for species that are disappearing."

What Chris especially likes about Earthwatch is that it becomes actively involved in the communities where it conducts work. "The project in Ghana is doing quite well," he says. "I've been reading that they stopped the hydroelectric dam because of Earthwatch people."

At the end of his freshman year at Harvard, Chris wrote a grant proposal that sent him back to Madagascar for three months. "I received funding from Harvard to start a community-education project there. It's vital," he says, "for any wildlife or environmental project, because without the support of the local community, and without the locals knowing what we're doing and why, it becomes an empty project."

His plan was to set up a "very casual, low-key kind of school," where for a few days each week, he taught in English to the locals. He focused on local environmental issues. Chris taught kids ages

Chris Golden and two of his students at the village school he organized in Madagascar (Chris Golden)

10 to 20, working in three different villages. In one of the larger villages there was an empty schoolhouse that was built by the French during the colonial period but was never used. It still is set up with desks and blackboards. Chris used the grant money to purchase paper, pencils, and books, and to pay an assistant who speaks Malagasy, the native language. Chris has a fair knowledge of French and Malagasy, as well.

Chris's school isn't the first community project in the villages. The project director, Luke Dollar, worked with a group of village women who were able to borrow money to build and run a lodge for tourists. "It's a sustainable method for them to be earning income for the women's group, while the locals become part of the research project." The women have already paid back the loan.

Just as Sara Finegan (see Chapter II) found her experience with Earthwatch rewarding, Chris Golden did, too. "It gave me the ability to try out what I'd always thought I wanted to do. It gave

me the ability to put the excitement I felt—from a
cials—into practical form. I got to see if I actually
So without Earthwatch I wouldn't have been able
Currently Chris is a junior at Harvard University majoring in bio-
logical anthropology. "But I'm using all of my electives to do ecology and conservation type stuff."

Earthwatch Institute
3 Clock Tower Place
Suite 100, Box 75
Maynard, MA 01754-0075
http://www.earthwatch.org
(888) 776-0188
(978) 461-2332
info@earthwatch.org

Blue Magruder, director of public affairs with Earthwatch, says,
"We are interested in those young people who are truly interested
in working with scientists and social scientists on projects. There
are some 760-plus mixed-generation projects we sponsor each
year, and 10 percent of those projects have young people on them.
It's a magical thing not to be segregated by age, and to be treated
as an adult and part of a team."

The cost of taking part in one of these projects ranges from
around $1,500 to $2,500, plus air travel. However, Magruder says,
"There are many scholarships available, and more than half our
young people qualify for them. We look for students who are
tough enough to backpack, who are interested in a varied experience, and who are curious and flexible and will enjoy doing real
science in an experiential setting." Earthwatch does not want
those who only want to add another notch to their college
applications.

Chris says that it's important to be flexible. "The food, the living conditions, the amount of work you will be doing—a lot of

times it can be tedious and repetitive. So you have to be interested in what you are doing. But you will be with people who are very passionate about what they are doing. It's an incredible experience being with people who are so willing to pay to volunteer to do something."

TRY A SUMMER WORK CAMP

If you have been spending your vacations going to summer camp and are looking for a different kind of experience, you might want to consider a work camp. Some are offered by organizations affiliated with religious groups. Others are privately funded. A work camp may operate in the United States, South America, Canada, Africa, or Europe—anywhere in the world where there is a need.

Dana Vetriecin from Highland Park, New Jersey, is no stranger to community service. "It is," she says, "a part of my life. It is something I do throughout the school year." After completing her junior year of high school, Dana signed on with the American Jewish Society for Service (AJSS).

The American Jewish Society for Service (AJSS) has been in business since 1950 and is directed toward juniors and seniors in high school, ages 15 to 17. Only 48 students are admitted each year, and they are placed in one of three work sites in the United States for a six-week period over the summer. Each group of eight boys and eight girls has two college counselors and one married couple.

Carl Brenner, director of AJSS, says, "We are invited into a community for a six-week period and work with whomever the host community wishes—underprivileged kids, the elderly, etc. The volunteers will do things such as put a new roof on someone's house, paint and fix up a home, help people actually build their homes, or run a day care facility or a summer camp." AJSS also teams up with Habitat for Humanity to work on new home construction.

Deconstructing houses

The mission given to Dana's group was unique. She was sent to Presque Isle in Aroostook County in Maine. All of the houses along a section of the Aroostook River had been destroyed by floods and ice jams the year before. The county had decided it was too dangerous for people to live along the river. At first they had planned to simply bulldoze the structures that were still standing and build a park, while resettling the dislocated families in another part of town. Instead, the 16 volunteers—eight boys and eight girls—dismantled the houses piece by piece, carefully saving anything that might be usable, from bricks and floorboards to kitchen sinks and bathtubs to fixtures and siding. Everything usable was donated to a materials bank run by Catholic Charities. They, in turn, sold the materials very cheaply to people who needed them to make improvements in their homes or to use in the new ones they were building.

"Someone, for example, who had never had a bathtub could get one for very little money," Dana says.

The project had far-reaching results. It saved the county hundreds of dollars in demolition costs, leaving more money to relocate the displaced families. And dozens of families would now be able to renovate and rebuild their houses.

Over the six-week period, Dana says, "we took down two trailer homes, a barn, and a house." Their site director was a local contractor who "had connections with everyone. He introduced us to the mayor, the governor, and we had a newspaper story written about us."

❏ Weekends were for fun:

The volunteers worked a full five-day week, Monday through Friday, and on Friday nights they met for a Shabbat service (the traditional Jewish Sabbath begins at sundown Friday night), which they wrote themselves. On the weekends the group would decide what kinds of activities they preferred. All decisions were by majority rule. "We went to Quebec one weekend and camping another," says Dana. Several times, the townspeople hosted the students for cookouts.

❏ Who signs up for AJSS work camps?

"Most of the students come from the Reform Jewish movement, primarily because we do not offer kosher meals and we use the weekends for travel and recreation," says Carl Brenner. However, it is not necessary to belong to a temple or a synagogue. Students can apply directly to AJSS. "Typically, the students are housed in a school building or in a synagogue," Brenner says. Dana's group lived in a nearby college dormitory, and there were five students living in a room that is normally a two-person dorm room.

❏ Good advice from a participant:

"You have to be the kind of person who likes to work hard and can live in a group situation. This can sometimes be difficult," Dana says. "There are often fights, which do get resolved, but not everyone can get along with everyone else. You do find your group, though. And you have to be open to change. You don't always know what you will be doing next, but it all works out. And you find your own group of friends. I didn't know anyone when I went there, and I managed to make five good friends."

❏ When to apply:

The cost of this program is $2,500 plus airfare and spending money. Brenner says, "This is a great experience in terms of group dynamics. It is a place where kids can make friends for life, and it is an experience of giving of yourself to people less fortunate." He noted that he himself was once a volunteer at an AJSS work camp site.

American Jewish Society for Service
15 East 26th Street, Room 1029
New York, NY 10010
(212) 683-6178
http://www.ajss.org/
info@ajss.org
Note: Only 48 students are accepted into the program each summer. It tends to get filled by October.

A challenging French experience

Johanna Kuhn-Osius spent her summer in France through a nonprofit organization called Volunteers for Peace. This organization was begun shortly after World War I and sets up work camps in partnership with a variety of host organizations throughout the world. The American headquarters are located in Belmont, Vermont.

Jennifer Brewer, one of three coordinators of the United States program, says that more than 400 volunteers from the United States go overseas and approximately 400 people from Europe come to the United States and Latin America each year. Although 80 percent of the volunteers are college students or older, Brewer notes, "We have several programs for high school students who are at least 15 years old. The countries that accept younger students into their programs are France, Germany, Turkey, and Russia." Brewer herself went to Russia on a VFP work camp when she was a teen. All volunteers pay their own transportation to the work camp site. They also pay a fee toward their room and board. The American students are divided up so that two or three Americans are working with up to 14 volunteers from other countries. English is primarily the language spoken, but it is a more intense experience if the students can speak the language of the host country.

❏ **Don't believe everything you read in the brochure:**

Johanna was sent to a work camp in Auvergne. "It was a very rural setting," she recalls. "There were 16 volunteers. We slept in two very large tents in a sheep meadow. There was one shower and two toilets for the 16 of us."

The sparse washing-up facilities and the tents were the least of the problems Johanna encountered. "I thought from the description in the brochure that I would be working with a group of 16 kids, and there would be two from each of the many countries. Instead, it turned out there were twelve French kids, two Americans, one from Italy, and one from Turkey."

Although Volunteers for Peace said that knowledge of the language of the host country wasn't necessary, it would have been very difficult if Johanna hadn't spoken French. The other American spoke only English. But on this site everyone spoke French—and it wasn't the kind of French you learn in school.

"The twelve French kids were mostly from group homes or were in foster care," says Johanna. "I have to say that my French increased dramatically. I certainly learned a lot of slang. And it is very different from speaking French in a school setting when you speak in their country with people your own age. The kids speak very fast and use a lot of slang and street talk. I had a bit of a rough time with the French kids. Most of them were there because they couldn't afford to do other things for the summer. Work camps are an inexpensive way to spend a vacation."

❏ **The quality of each work camp can vary:**

Jennifer says up front that Volunteers for Peace is a very decentralized organization. "Some work camps are better organized than others. There are more than 800 programs to choose from, ranging from laying out a student equestrian center to social programs with the elderly or refugees to children's day camps to remodeling houses to organic farming and street theater."

❑ Doing work that is useful:

Despite the difficulties with some of the kids, Johanna enjoyed much of her adventure. It happened that the other American girl lives just twenty blocks from Johanna in Manhattan—and they have stayed in touch. Also, the work itself was important. Next to the sheep meadow where the students were housed was a chateau, originally built during the early Middle Ages. The students were restoring and rebuilding it so that eventually it would become a vacation retreat for people who are differently abled. Johanna's group was the second one to work on the project, and there would be others after she left.

"To do this sort of work camp, you have to be very tolerant," says Johanna. "You never know what will happen. We laid tiles in the kitchen of the chateau, put cement in cracks in the stone basin, which, when it is all completed, will be used as a swimming pool. We laid bricks and dug rain ditches in the forest. Another work crew dug a duck pond, while the ducks and geese and other animals milled around. When it rained, we worked inside the chateau, scraping and sanding floors, painting, and tiling."

The work week was Monday through Friday, with a half day on Friday. Bedtime was 11 P.M. This was strictly enforced because, although the tents had electricity, it was controlled from the chateau, "and at 11 P.M., they would turn off the electricity. If you tried to use a flashlight, the beam would attract all the bugs."

❑ Roll with the punches:

On weekends, the students hiked in nearby forests, and on Bastille Day (July 14), they walked into the village for the celebration. "We walked and hiked everywhere because there was only one car for the 16 of us. I wouldn't want to hide the fact that this work camp was unstructured," Johanna says. "But if you know this beforehand, you can deal with it. Volunteers for Peace is a very good program. They can't control the organizations overseas. I am the kind of person who doesn't need organization to have a good time, and I didn't need the security of other Americans. But some of the time it was rough. Many of the kids would talk about their lives, and some of them came from areas where there were gangs, and so forth.

"If you do Volunteers for Peace, you need to have an open attitude. Maybe the next tour will be different." Yes, Johanna intends to sign up for another VFP work camp—this time with an older group. "It all depends on the partnership organization and the particular group to which you get assigned. And I did get to meet real French people."

Volunteers for Peace publishes an annual directory every April giving a rough outline of the various programs. After a student registers, he or she will receive more detailed information.

A typical renovation project at a Volunteers for Peace summer work camp in Germany (Katrina Richter)

Volunteers for Peace
1034 Tiffany Road
Belmont, VT 05730-0202
(802) 259-2759
(802) 259-2922
vfp@vfp.org
http://www.vfp.org

Community service right at home

Laura Artim says she was "just a regular high school student concentrating on getting into her first choice college." She did well in
sports and hung out with her friends, and her grades were excellent.
But she felt that "something was missing" in her life. So she decided
to check out volunteering at an organization called VIVE la Casa—a
refugee shelter in downtown Buffalo, just a 25-minute drive from her
home. "I signed up at my school (which offers an entire menu of volunteering possibilities), and had an interview with the director of
VIVE." After Laura filled out a form that gave the director an opportunity to find out what her interests were, she was taken on as a volunteer. "VIVE does some very interesting work with all kinds of
refugees, who are not necessarily legal immigrants."

At first, while she was still going to school, she worked in the
office one day a week, doing some paperwork and working on a
fund-raising project to get baby items donated. "And," she said, "I
actually got to go on the radio. I knew this radio DJ, so I went on
the radio and spoke about the need for donations." After the spots
aired, there were a lot of donations over the next few weeks.

During the summer after she graduated from high school, Laura
volunteered at VIVE two days a week. The other days she worked
at a business owned by the father of one of her friends. Laura
helped with a play the residents put on, and she went shoppin^
with the residents for food that was prepared for an internatio
dinner. "And I wrote for their newsletter."

Other times, Laura worked on various craft projects with the children. "Sometimes it was crazy and sometimes it was nice."

Most of the refugees who come to VIVE eventually wind up in Canada. Besides offering these people a temporary safe place to live, VIVE provides counseling, sets up appointments with Canadian and U.S. immigration, and helps people acculturate to a new country. People stay for a few weeks or for several months, and they come from all over the world, from places such as Central America, West Africa, and Pakistan. VIVE, which is part of the Episcopal Community Service, does not turn anyone away. Each year they help thousands of men, women, and children find a safe haven.

This experience made Laura appreciate how difficult it was for people in distress to find a safe place to live. "It became a part of me to make sure I was doing something useful each day." She says she felt she became less self-centered. "I started reading the newspapers and signed up for classes that had to do with global issues." Her intention now is to study international relations at the University of Chicago. (Yes, she did get into her first-choice college.)

VIVE la Casa, Inc.
50 Wyoming Avenue
Buffalo, NY 14215
(716) 892-4354
www.vivelacasa.org
vive@buffnet.net

̄ ̇+\ year—a community service experience

,rything I want to do," says Moira Heiges of

̇al

. graduated from St. Ignatius High School in
ded to postpone college for a year and work on

a project to aid "at risk" youth. In City Year, which is funded by AmeriCorps, Moira led a team of eight people who worked on the near north side of Chicago in a community that was "under resourced." The team members were a diverse group—four African Americans, two Caucasians, two Latinos, and Moira.

It was a challenging experience, and not everything worked out according to plan. "We were, for example, supposed to be setting up an after school program in a high school, but the kids wouldn't come to it. They didn't feel safe there, so we ended up doing something else." Moira and her team decided to go to a middle school, where they first spent time meeting with the principal and teachers. Here they began to work directly with the students in the classrooms and got to know the kids. By the third month, Moira's group had established a relationship with the children, and they were able to set up different community service projects every Saturday. "We'd do community clean ups and organized community gardens. We went to a shelter for families affected by AIDS and painted a meeting room for them, and we sorted clothing. And," Moira says, "we'd take fun trips and go ice skating and visit museums."

Once her team got into the swing of things, they organized a tutoring program with the kids who finally did come to an after-school program. During the day they went into the classrooms and "taught life skills that concentrated on building self-esteem, and what to do when someone offers you drugs."

Moira admits that there were difficulties with the City Year program. "Everyone comes for different reasons, and everybody has strong opinions, and there's not enough money to do the things you want to do. And often the team leaders don't get good programs planned for them, and [even if there's a good program] you don't have enough money to carry it out, and you have to wear a uniform." The uniforms actually turn out to be a good thing, because the volunteers are recognized by the community as good people who are there to help. "And," Moira continues, "you're five minutes late for a staff meeting and someone wants to discipline you!" Additionally, in order to do the kinds of things they wanted to do with the children, each team had to raise its own money by writing letters to businesses to get donations. In Moira's group, there were only two people who felt comfortable doing that— writing letters, speaking to corporate sponsors, and doing other types of fund-raising.

Despite these challenges, Moira felt "like a million dollars at the end of the year. I felt like I had just done something pretty big, because I knew that City Year hadn't been around for that many years, and I knew that we'd strengthened our site, and we made new relationships with schools. And, man, I'd survived this! I felt pretty strong. I wasn't scared at all to go to college. I'd done something really incredible."

One thing that pleased her was that the people in the neighborhood knew that Moira and her team were "good people who were doing something with the kids, and that we were part of something good." Although her team members worked five days a week, as team leader, she usually worked six.

Moira received a stipend of $200 a week and was able to save some money because she lived at home. AmeriCorps also gave her $5,000 at the end of the year toward her first year's college tuition.

"City Year was a chance for me to feel that I was really doing service full-time. For an 18-year-old, that was terrific." And she knows that her project will continue working in the schools she and her team set up.

City Year, Inc.
285 Columbus Avenue
Boston, MA 02116
info@cityyear.org
http://www.cityyear.org

A FINAL WORD

All reputable organizations will publish a list of participants with addresses and phone numbers from the previous year. Before you sign on with a program, call a couple of people and ask questions. As is obvious from those whose stories appear in this chapter, you have to be prepared to work in a variety of unusual situations. It would appear that having a sense of humor, as well as a lot of mosquito repellent, is a great help. You can look on the Web to find many other summer programs that have a community service component. Or, if you belong to a church or synagogue, check out community service opportunities within your religious organization. Be sure to ask to speak to at least three kids who have signed up with these organizations within the past year or two.

Chapter VII

Can I Become a Real Man or Woman by Joining the Military?

A TELEVISION COMMERCIAL SHOWS A RECENT HIGH SCHOOL GRADU-ATE TELLING HIS DAD HE'S GOING TO JOIN THE ARMY AND LEARN ALL ABOUT COMPUTERS. "I'm proud of you, son," his father says. "Be all that you can be," the television blares. "Join the U.S. Army."

The U.S. Air Force ad shows a handsome officer putting on his flight helmet. As he jumps into a sleek F-14 fighter plane and revs the engine, he waves to a beautiful girl. Then he flies off into the sunset. "Join the Air Force," you are urged. "Become a fighter pilot." A U.S. Navy recruiter comes to your school in his crisp dress uniform and extols the virtues of a naval career. "If you join the Navy, you'll see the world." And of course, the United States Marines are always "looking for a few good men." You could be one of them.

"Well," you may think, "perhaps I ought to consider a hitch in the military." After all, when you turn 18, if you are male, you are obligated to register for selective service, even though at this time there is no active draft.

Perhaps your father, brother, uncle, aunt, grandfather, or other relative served in the military. You've heard them reminisce about the "good old days." They gloss over the bad parts and talk about the different countries they were sent to, the friends they made, the good times they had—and of fulfilling an obligation to their country. One of them may slap you on the back and say, "The Army really straightened me out," or, "I learned discipline in the Navy."

Perhaps a relative went to college under the GI Bill or got an ROTC scholarship. Getting some money to pay for your college education by giving your country a couple of years of your life doesn't sound so bad. It may even turn out that a military career is really what you are looking for. You also need to realize, though, that by joining a branch of the military you are signing on to give your life, if need be, for your country. That is an awesome and serious commitment to make.

SOME GREAT FINANCIAL DEALS

There are numerous financial incentives available to those who join the military.

1. Reserve Officers' Training Corps (ROTC) scholarships are sponsored by the U.S. Army, Navy, Air Force, and Marines in more than 300 colleges and universities. According to Lieutenant. Colonel Michael Merola, who is in charge of ROTC at Cornell University, in return for serving eight years in either the Reserves or on active duty after college graduation, plus about ten hours of classroom and field training each week during your four years of college, you can apply for substantial financial aid. For each of the four years you attend college, you may be eligible for a scholarship that covers your entire tuition. You will also be given a stipend of $250 to $400 per month, plus an additional allowance for books and fees. If you are admitted to one of the 25 supertier universities, such as Cornell or Syracuse University, you can also apply for a $20,000 scholarship. These are highly competitive. More than 30,000 students apply each year. If you win a scholarship and then drop out of ROTC, you will have to pay back the scholarship money but not the monthly stipend. "Very few people drop out of ROTC," says Merola.

2. If you join a branch of the military and get it written into your contract at the time of your enlistment, you can become eligible for a four-year education absolutely free, plus living allowances, thanks to Uncle Sam. Of course, there are tough qualifying exams to pass. One Army recruiter said that these scholarships often go begging because so few people apply for them at the time of enlistment. Once you are through with your basic training, you will attend the college of your choice, and you can wear civilian clothes. However, upon college graduation, you will owe the military two, four, or eight years of service. After some further training, you will have officer's rank.

3. The National Guard will help you out while you are in school, if you pledge six years worth of weekends and summers. You will get $190 a month in college benefits, plus $130 a month in pay. In many states Guards get free tuition in public colleges.

4. If you enlist in the military before you go to college and agree to kick in $1,200 from your paycheck, the U.S. Army, Navy, Marines, or Air Force will boost that amount by another $13,200. Upon an honorable discharge, you will be entitled to a tax-free monthly installment of $400 a month (for nine months) for four years of college.

5. While you are in the armed services, there are many opportunities for you to attend college where you are stationed. Some of these college courses are free, and others are 75 percent covered.

WAIT!

Before you rush down to your friendly recruitment office and sign up, do some serious investigating. Be absolutely certain that you know what you are getting yourself into. Trying to get out of the military if you decide it doesn't suit you isn't as simple as dropping a course you don't like. The military can be a sensible choice. But if you don't get all the facts before you enlist, you may wind up a very unhappy person for the next two, four, or eight years.

ENLISTMENT/REENLISTMENT DOCUMENT
ARMED FORCES OF THE UNITED STATES
PRIVACY ACT STATEMENT

AUTHORITY: 5 USC 3331; 32 USC 708; 44 USC 708 and 3101; 10 USC 133, 265, 275, 504, 508, 510, 591, 672(d), 678, 837, 1007, 1071 through 1087; 1168, 1169, 1475 through 1480, 1553, 2107, 2122, 3012, 5031, 8012, 8033, 8496, and 9411; 14 USC 351 and 632; and Executive Order 9397, November 1943 (SSN).

PRINCIPAL PURPOSE(S): To record enlistment or reenlistment into the U.S. Armed Forces. This information becomes a part of the subject's military personnel records which are used to document promotion, reassignment, training, medical support, and other personnel management actions. The purpose of soliciting the SSN is for positive identification.

ROUTINE USE(S): This form becomes a part of the Service's Enlisted Master File and Field Personnel File. All uses of the form are internal to the relevant Service.

DISCLOSURE: Voluntary; however, failure to furnish personal identification information may negate the enlistment/reenlistment application.

A. ENLISTEE/REENLISTEE IDENTIFICATION DATA

1. NAME *(Last, First, Middle)*	2. SOCIAL SECURITY NUMBER
3. HOME OF RECORD *(Street, City, State, ZIP Code)*	4. PLACE OF ENLISTMENT/REENLISTMENT *(Mil. Installation, City, State)*

5. DATE OF ENLISTMENT/ REENLISTMENT *(YYYYMMDD)*	6. DATE OF BIRTH *(YYYYMMDD)*	7. PREV MIL SVC UPON ENL/REENLIST	YEARS	MONTHS	DAYS
		a. TOTAL ACTIVE MILITARY SERVICE			
		b. TOTAL INACTIVE MILITARY SERVICE			

B. AGREEMENTS

8. I am enlisting/reenlisting in the United States *(list branch of service)* _____ this date for _____ years and _____ weeks beginning in pay grade _____. The additional details of my enlistment/reenlistment are in Section C and Annex(es) _____.

a. FOR ENLISTMENT IN A DELAYED ENTRY/ENLISTMENT PROGRAM (DEP):
I understand that I will be ordered to active duty as a Reservist unless I report to the place shown in item 4 above by *(list date (YYYYMMDD))* _____ for enlistment in the Regular component of the United States *(list branch of service)* _____ for not less than _____ years and _____ weeks. My enlistment in the DEP is in a nonpay status. I understand that my period in the DEP is NOT creditable for pay purposes upon entry into a pay status. However, I also understand that this time is counted toward fulfillment of my military service obligation or commitment. I must maintain my current qualifications and keep my recruiter informed of any changes in my physical or dependency status, moral qualifications, and mailing address.

b. REMARKS: *(If none, so state.)*

c. The agreements in this section and attached annex(es) are all the promises made to me by the Government. **ANYTHING ELSE ANYONE HAS PROMISED ME IS NOT VALID AND WILL NOT BE HONORED.**

(Initials of Enlistee/Reenlistee) _____   *(Continued on reverse side.)*

DD FORM 4/1, AUG 1998 (EG)   PREVIOUS EDITION IS OBSOLETE.   USAPA V1.00

Enlistment/Reenlistment Document Armed Forces of the United States, page 1

C. PARTIAL STATEMENT OF EXISTING UNITED STATES LAWS

9. **FOR ALL ENLISTEES OR REENLISTEES:** Many laws, regulations, and military customs will govern my conduct and require me to do things a civilian does not have to do. The following statements are not promises or guarantees of any kind. They explain some of the present laws affecting the Armed Forces which I cannot change but which Congress can change at any time.

a. My enlistment is more than an employment agreement. As a member of the Armed Forces of the United States, I will be:

(1) Required to obey all lawful orders and perform all assigned duties.

(2) Subject to separation during or at the end of my enlistment. If my behavior fails to meet acceptable military standards, I may be discharged and given a certificate for less than honorable service, which may hurt my future job opportunities and my claim for veteran's benefits.

(3) Subject to the military justice system, which means, among other things, that I may be tried by military courts-martial.

(4) Required upon order to serve in combat or other hazardous situations.

(5) Entitled to receive pay, allowances, and other benefits as provided by law and regulation.

b. Laws and regulataions that govern military personnel may change without notice to me. Such changes may affect my status, pay, allowances, benefits, and responsibilities as a member of the Armed Forces **REGARDLESS** of the provisions of this enlistment/reenlistment document.

c. In the event of war, my enlistment in the Armed Forces continues until six (6) months after the war ends, unless my enlistment is ended sooner by the President of the United States.

10. MILITARY SERVICE OBLIGATION FOR ALL MEMBERS OF THE ACTIVE AND RESERVE COMPONENTS, INCLUDING THE NATIONAL GUARD.

a. **FOR ALL ENLISTEES:** If this is my initial enlistment, I must serve a total of eight (8) years. Any part of that service not served on active duty must be served in a Reserve Component unless I am sooner discharged.

b. If I am a member of a Reserve Component of an Armed Force at the beginning of a period of war or national emergency declared by Congress, or if I become a member during that period, my military service may be extended without my consent until six (6) months after the end of that period of war.

c. As a member of a Reserve Component, in time of war or national emergency declared by the Congress, I may be required to serve on active duty (other than for training) for the entire period of the war or emergency and for six (6) months after its end.

d. As a member of the Ready Reserve I may be required to perform active duty or active duty for training without my consent (other than as provided in item 8 of this document) as follows:

(1) in time of national emergency declared by the President of the United States, I may be ordered to active duty (other than for training) for not more than 24 consecutive months.

(2) I may be ordered to active duty for 24 months, and my enlistment may be extended so I can complete 24 months of active duty, if:

(a) I am not assigned to, or participating satisfactorily in, a unit of the Ready Reserve; and

(b) I have not met my Reserve obligation; and

(c) I have not served on active duty for a total of 24 months.

(3) I may be ordered to perform additional active duty training for not more than 45 days if I have not fulfilled my military service obligation and fail in any year to perform the required training duty satisfactorily. If the failure occurs during the last year of my required membership in the Ready Reserve, my enlistment may be extended until I perform that additional duty, but not for more than six months.

(4) When determined by the President that it is necessary to support any operational mission, I may be ordered to active duty as prescribed by law, if I am a member of the Selected Reserve.

11. FOR ENLISTEES/REENLISTEES IN THE NAVY, MARINE CORPS, OR COAST GUARD: I understand that if I am serving on a naval vessel in foreign waters, and my enlistment expires, I will be returned to the United States for discharge as soon as possible consistent with my desires. However, if retained on active duty is essential to the public interest, I understand that I may be retained on active duty until the vessel returns to the United States. If I am retained under these circumstances, I understand I will be discharged not later than 30 days after my return to the United States; and, that except in time of war, I will be entitled to an increase in basic pay of 25 percent from the date my enlistment expires to the date of my discharge.

12. FOR ALL MALE APPLICANTS: Completion of this form constitutes registration with the Selective Service System in accordance with the Military Selective Service Act. Incident thereto the Department of Defense may transmit my name, permanent address, military address, Social Security Number, and birthdate to the Selective Service System for recording as evidence of the registration.

DD FORM 4/1 (BACK), AUG 1998   USAPA V1.00

Enlistment/Reenlistment Document Armed Forces of the United States, page 2

NAME OF ENLISTEE/REENLISTEE *(Last, First, Middle)*	SOCIAL SECURITY NO. OF ENLISTEE/REENLISTEE

D. CERTIFICATION AND ACCEPTANCE

13a. My acceptance for enlistment is based on the information I have given in my application for enlistment. If any of that information is false or incorrect, this enlistment may be voided or terminated administratively by the Government or I may be tried by a Federal, civilian, or military court and, if found guilty, may be punished.

I CERTIFY THAT I HAVE CAREFULLY READ THIS DOCUMENT. ANY QUESTIONS I HAD WERE EXPLAINED TO MY SATISFACTION. I FULLY UNDERSTAND THAT ONLY THOSE AGREEMENTS IN SECTION B OF THIS DOCUMENT OR RECORDED ON THE ATTACHED ANNEX(ES) WILL BE HONORED. ANY OTHER PROMISES OR GUARANTEES MADE TO ME BY ANYONE ARE WRITTEN BELOW: *(If none, X "NONE" and initial.)* [ ] NONE _____ *(Initials of enlistee/reenlistee)*

b. SIGNATURE OF ENLISTEE/REENLISTEE	c. DATE SIGNED *(YYYYMMDD)*

14. SERVICE REPRESENTATIVE CERTIFICATION

a. On behalf of the United States *(list branch of service)* _____ ,
I accept this applicant for enlistment. I have witnessed the signature in item 13b to this document. I certify that I have explained that only those agreements in Section B of this form and in the attached Annex(es) will be honored, and any other promises made by any person are not effective and will not be honored.

b. NAME *(Last, First, Middle)*	c. PAY GRADE	d. UNIT/COMMAND NAME
e. SIGNATURE	f. DATE SIGNED *(YYYYMMDD)*	g. UNIT/COMMAND ADDRESS *(City, State, ZIP Code)*

E. CONFIRMATION OF ENLISTMENT OR REENLISTMENT

15. IN THE ARMED FORCES EXCEPT THE NATIONAL GUARD (ARMY OR AIR):
I, _____ , do solemnly swear (or affirm) that I will support and defend the Constitution of the United States against all enemies; that I will bear true faith and allegiance to the same; and that I will obey the orders of the President of the United States and the orders of the officers appointed over me, according to regulations and the Uniform Code of Military Justice. So help me God.

16. IN THE NATIONAL GUARD (ARMY OR AIR):
I, _____ , do solemnly swear (or affirm) that I will support and defend the Constitution of the United States and the State of _____ against all enemies, foreign and domestic; that I will bear true faith and allegiance to the same; and that I will obey the orders of the President of the United States and the Governor of _____ and the orders of the officers appointed over me, according to law and regulations. So help me God.

17. IN THE NATIONAL GUARD (ARMY OR AIR):
I do hereby acknowledge to have voluntarily enlisted/reenlisted this _____ day of _____ , _____ in the _____ National Guard and as a Reserve of the United States *(list branch of service)* _____ with membership in the _____ National Guard of the United States for a period of _____ years, _____ months, _____ days, under the conditions prescribed by law, unless sooner discharged by proper authority.

18.a. SIGNATURE OF ENLISTEE/REENLISTEE	b. DATE SIGNED *(YYYYMMDD)*

19. ENLISTMENT/REENLISTMENT OFFICER CERTIFICATION

a. The above oath was administered, subscribed, and duly sworn to (or affirmed) before me this date.

b. NAME *(Last, First, Middle)*	c. PAY GRADE	d. UNIT/COMMAND NAME
e. SIGNATURE	f. DATE SIGNED *(YYYYMMDD)*	g. UNIT/COMMAND ADDRESS *(City, State, ZIP Code)*

DD FORM 4/2, AUG 1998   PREVIOUS EDITION IS OBSOLETE.   USAPA V1.00

Enlistment/Reenlistment Document Armed Forces of the United States, page 3

| NAME OF ENLISTEE/REENLISTEE (Last, First, Middle) | SOCIAL SECURITY NO. OF ENLISTEE/REENLISTEE |

F. DISCHARGE FROM/DELAYED ENTRY/ENLISTMENT PROGRAM

20a. I request to be discharged from the Delayed Entry/Enlistment Program (DEP) and enlisted in the Regular

Component of the United States (list branch of service) _____ for a period of

_____ years and _____ weeks. No changes have been made to my enlistment options OR

if changes were made they are recorded on Annex(es) _____

_____ which replace(s) Annex(es) _____ .

| b. SIGNATURE OF DELAYED ENTRY/ENLISTMENT PROGRAM ENLISTEE | c. DATE SIGNED (YYYYMMDD) |

G. APPROVAL AND ACCEPTANCE BY SERVICE REPRESENTATIVE

21. SERVICE REPRESENTATIVE CERTIFICATION

a. This enlistee is discharged from the Reserve Component shown in item 8 and is accepted for enlistment in the

Regular Component of the United States (list branch of service) _____ in pay grade _____ .

| b. NAME (Last, First, Middle) | c. PAY GRADE | d. UNIT/COMMAND NAME |
| e. SIGNATURE | f. DATE SIGNED (YYYYMMDD) | g. UNIT/COMMAND ADDRESS (City, State, ZIP Code) |

H. CONFIRMATION OF ENLISTMENT OR REENLISTMENT

22a. IN A REGULAR COMPONENT OF THE ARMED FORCES:

I, _____ do solemnly swear (or affirm) that I will support and

defend the Constitution of the United States against all enemies, foreign and domestic; that I will bear true faith

and allegiance to the same; and that I will obey the orders of the President of the United States and the orders of

the officers appointed over me, according to regulations and the Uniform Code of Military Justice. So help me

God.

| b. SIGNATURE OF ENLISTEE/REENLISTEE | b. DATE SIGNED (YYYYMMDD) |

23. ENLISTMENT OFFICER CERTIFICATION

a. The above oath was administered, subscribed, and duly sworn to (or affirmed) before me this date.

| b. NAME (Last, First, Middle) | c. PAY GRADE | d. UNIT/COMMAND NAME |
| e. SIGNATURE | f. DATE SIGNED (YYYYMMDD) | g. UNIT/COMMAND ADDRESS (City, State, ZIP Code) |

DD FORM 4/3, AUG 1998   PREVIOUS EDITION IS OBSOLETE.   USAPA V1.00

Enlistment/Reenlistment Document Armed Forces of the United States, page 4

People who have served in the military will tell you that your attitude will determine a great deal about your life in the service.

LOOK BEFORE YOU LEAP

Tim Ryan of Groton, New York, had been admitted to the University of Delaware when he was just 16 years old, but he wasn't very motivated to do well. "I did manage to maintain a 2.8 average, but to tell the truth, I didn't go to classes very much, and I decided I was wasting my time."

Tim came back home after his first year and bounced around at various jobs for the next couple of years. When he was 18 he took the Armed Services Vocational Aptitude Battery (ASVAB). "I've always been a good test taker, and I did real well on it."

> **"I didn't go to classes very much, and I decided I was wasting my time."**

The ASVAB is given at your local high school by a test administrator from the federal government. It is free, takes about three hours, and requires no specialized knowledge. It does not obligate you in any way to join the military. However, once you've taken it, you can be certain that you will be called by recruiters from all branches of the service—especially if you score high.

Tim recalls how much he liked to play war when he was a little kid. "But I didn't have any concept of what that was like. I thought it was all Hollywood World War II movies. All of the glory and none of the blood."

While Tim was thinking about this, he was called by an Air Force recruiter who told him his test scores were great. He told Tim that one of the good things about the Air Force is that "it builds character and discipline."

"And," Tim says, "I thought, 'Boy! I could really use a shot of discipline in my life.'" And here was the Air Force offering him a lifeline. He signed up for four years.

Tim used the computer in the recruitment headquarters to look up the many specialties the Air Force offers. "I wanted to go into intelligence," he says. "But there were no openings."

> ## "I could really use a shot of discipline in my life."

The recruiter told Tim that there might be openings in six months. "So if you go in now under a 'general category,' with your test scores, I can almost assure you that you will get what you want."

Tim was swayed by what the recruiter said. He figured that with his year of college Russian and his great test scores, he was just the man Air Force intelligence was looking for. So he signed his contract under something called "general category."

His contract didn't say anything about being trained for intelligence.

Did Tim do something foolish? Yes, indeed. He soon learned that without a guaranteed contract, he would never make it into intelligence training. What Uncle Sam was after was his body, not his mind.

HOW TO AVOID MISTAKES WHEN ENLISTING IN THE MILITARY

The time to avoid making mistakes is before you sign your contract. Consider the following before you enlist:

1. Forget about all the movies and TV shows you've seen about World War II, the Korean War, Vietnam, or the Gulf War.

2. Remember that the advertisements for the military are just that—advertisements meant to get you to believe you can be trained for something very special right out of high school.

No high school graduate can become a pilot. The television commercial doesn't tell you that you have to be a college graduate in a technical field such as engineering to even be considered for flight school. Then you have to spend time being trained as an officer, plus 110 hours as a pilot. According to former New York State veterans counselor Harry DeLibero, only 10 percent of those who are admitted into flight school ever succeed.

Very few jobs in the military are actually transferable to civilian life. There isn't much call for someone who can help build a bomb. There isn't much call for someone who can drive a tank. DeLibero notes, "The military is not a college. They are not going to train you for civilian work." Although it is true that every position in the military has a civilian job title, most of those titles are not accurate. Fully 30 percent of the job titles have no true civilian equivalent.

Much of the enlistee's work will center around carrying a rifle, pulling guard duty, picking up cigarette butts, and mindless drudgery.

You have to remember the purpose of going into the military is to learn how to kill. "Don't," cautions DeLibero, "ever forget that."

3. If the commercial or booklet says you can "go into computers," find out just what that means. If you are not careful, you will wind up sweeping out the room where they keep the computers. It doesn't mean that the Army will train you top to bottom with everything you ever wanted to know about computers, unless it is specifically written into the contract you sign.

4. The only ad that is realistic is the one in which there are soldiers driving tanks. As a high school graduate, you can learn to drive a tank, if that's what you want to do. But you will not spend all of your time doing that. You will do a lot of policing the grounds.

5. Read your contract, and don't be prejudiced by the person talking to you. Recruiters are trained to talk with 17- and 18-year-olds. They know exactly what to say to make you feel very important—and they have a monthly quota to fill.

6. Do not sign anything right there in the recruiter's office. Take your time. Take the contract home and have at least one other adult person go over your it with you. If it doesn't say exactly what you want it to say, DON'T SIGN IT. Go back to the recruiter's office with your notes, and get the contract changed. Then take the second version home with you and have a responsible person go over it with you.

7. You don't have to sign up until the area in which you are interested becomes available. It's fine to wait several months or even a year for a specialty that really suits you. In the meantime you can get yourself some technical skills, perhaps by signing up for a course or two at your local community college.

8. There are some definite advantages to joining the military as long as you have a clear idea of what you are getting yourself into. The best advice is to take yourself very, very seriously. It is going to be your life on the line. Every day for the next several years you will wake up and still be a member of the armed forces. Every day for the next several years, you run the risk of being sent to war. You owe it to yourself, and to the branch of the service you choose, to see that your special talents are used to the fullest.

CAREFUL RESEARCH PAYS OFF

Like Tim Ryan, Steve Yatko from Clark Summit, Pennsylvania, had always been interested in the military. "My father," says Steve, "is a civilian who works for the government." Steve always believed that serving his country in some capacity was in the cards for him. Steve dreamed of becoming a pilot. "I've wanted to fly ever since I was a baby," he says. In fact, he obtained his private

Be Sure Your Contract Says What You Want It to Say

➤ The contract you sign is inviolate and immutable. You can't change it, regardless of what the recruiter says.

➤ Unless they are preparing you for some specific job (say you are fluent in Serbo-Croatian, Chinese, or Arabic, or you play the trumpet), you will be an ordinary recruit.

➤ If you are 18, have just finished high school, and have never signed a contract before, you are in a very vulnerable position.

➤ If, after you have been trained for a specific job, that job isn't available, you will be offered a different job. You have the right to refuse it and leave the service with an honorable discharge. However, until your discharge comes through, you can be subjected to a lot of harassment. It may not be pleasant.

pilot's license before he turned 16. Steve believes that the "military is the best place to get flight training. And after training, you can fly the world's best aircraft. I want to do that. All of my life, flying has been a constant."

But Steve had another reason for becoming a military man. "I was always a B student. My SAT scores were 1130. I looked upon myself as an average student. There are millions of people just like me and millions of people who are smarter than I am." Steve knew that he'd have to do something outstanding in order to qualify for an ROTC scholarship.

At 16 Steve had put together a lot of things about himself: his assessment of his scholastic abilities; his desire to be of service to his country; his love of flying; his desire for a college education with a major in government. Then he talked to lots of people, both in the military and out. "I got a lot of opinions and ideas on different routes I might examine."

Steve decided the Navy had the most to offer him. He found a special Navy prep school called BOOST, designed specifically to train future naval officers. In order to get into BOOST, you must agree to join the Navy. "If you pass their very stiff courses in chemistry, calculus, physics, English, writing, and reading," Steve says, "you get a scholarship to an ROTC school or to the Naval Academy in Annapolis."

Steve took the ASVAB and did well enough to be admitted to BOOST. "All I had to do then was to enlist and join the Navy." Just after Steve celebrated his 17th birthday, he found himself 3,000 miles from home at boot camp in San Diego, California. He knew that if he flunked out of the BOOST program, he would owe the Navy seven years of active duty. And there is a 50 percent dropout rate from BOOST.

But Steve did well in the program. He was admitted into the Naval Academy. But after a year, he felt he was not getting what he wanted out of Annapolis. BOOST had promised Steve (in writing) a college education either at the Academy or at a college with an ROTC program. He transferred to a college in upstate New York.

Steve had no guarantee that he would make it into flight school after graduation. "I think the only thing that is certain in life is death," he says. But he passed all of his tests and is on his way to flight training.

THE COAST GUARD BECKONS

Remember Lucy Morris from Chapter 1? She also had been in love with flying and had made flying the centerpiece of her life. Like Steve, she had gotten her private pilot's license while still in high school. She had even obtained her flight instructor's license a few years later, but she was looking for more challenges. "I would like to teach flying at a different level than what is taught at the little airports. I'm interested in the whole psychology of the human being as it relates to flying."

While Lucy was casting about for a way to move on, she says, "I woke up one morning and said, 'Coast Guard.' And I called up a recruiter and got information. I enjoy helping people, and I enjoy listening to people." It seemed to her that all the things she liked to do were things that were done in the Coast Guard. She liked the idea of helping people during natural disasters. "If I did that sort of thing on a volunteer basis, I'd have to take time off from my job. But as a Coast Guard member, I'd be getting paid for doing things that are important." She also liked the pay scale. "I guess it is around $900 a month, plus room and board. As someone who has always been extremely broke, I'm going to be very cautious with the money I earn. I've got a lot of student loans to pay off, and I'll try to use my money wisely."

There were several things that were worrisome to Lucy. "I spent a lot of time going over the time commitment in my mind—four years of active duty and four years of inactive service. It did scare me. But I talked to a lot of people and found that the general public image of the Coast Guard was very good. And that people who are in the Coast Guard are generally happy with what they do." Lucy also liked the fact that she has found virtually no discrimination against women in the Coast Guard. The one time an instructor made a comment about "all you guys," he immediately corrected himself. "I meant men and women," he said. (The Coast Guard has accepted women since 1970.)

IF YOU BECOME DISILLUSIONED

Even though Tim Ryan soon realized he'd made a mistake when he didn't sign up for a specific job, he decided to save his money and try to enjoy himself for the four years he was in the Air Force. His straightforward attitude and high spirits landed him a job in communications training. His job was to fly with a crew into an area to set up advanced air bases. "In case of a war," he says, "we'd have to fly in and set up the communications system." Fortunately for Tim, there was no war during his years in the service.

For the first year and a half, Tim had a good time in the Air Force. By the end of his second year, "I just became more and more disillusioned." It wasn't anything definite. It was more a matter of observing some things that were happening to his friends when they got into trouble. Some of them received less-than-honorable discharges.

"A less-than-honorable discharge," says counselor DeLibero, "is very serious. You can never go back in the service to reverse this. Any time you apply for a job, you may be asked if you have ever served in the military. When you answer 'yes,' a prospective employer may ask to see discharge papers. The unfortunate thing is," DeLibero says, "that if the young person never had gone into the service, he or she wouldn't have that prejudice against them. If, for example, your discharge says something like 'inability to adapt to military life' because you didn't want to be there, or you showed up late for inspection, you probably won't get the [civilian] job."

> ## "A less-than-honorable discharge is very serious."

Tim had also done a lot of thinking about what he wanted to learn in college. He was anxious to get back to school. So he began a dialogue with his commander. He told him how strongly he felt about getting out of the Air Force. This didn't please his commander, who was a career officer. Career personnel tend to view those who enlist for a short period of time, and who complain about the military life, with little or no respect. Tim's commander sent him to see a psychiatrist. After some time, however, even his commander recognized that Tim was sincere in his desire to get out. Because there were many people who wished to get into the Air Force at that time, Tim was able to leave with an honorable discharge after two years.

If Tim had used his dissatisfaction as an excuse to get into trouble, he would have risked a less-than-honorable discharge, and the stain on his record would have followed him for the rest of his life.

Tim was fortunate. He had over $6,000 in his education fund, plus $2,500 in savings. And he didn't feel all that negative about his experience.

"If anyone ever asked me about going into the Air Force, I'd say, 'Go ahead.' I would tell you to go for it." Among the things he remembers best are the friends he made and the cities he got to see. When Tim got out of the service, he enrolled at SUNY Cortland and graduated with a degree in philosophy.

LEARNING TO TAKE RESPONSIBILITY FOR HIMSELF

John Weeldreyer was 18 when he joined the Navy. He was one of those kids who just "floated through high school" not knowing what he wanted to do with himself he says. "I didn't have the money or the parental support at that time. And I was always blaming other people for what went wrong in my life. When I was in high school, I dropped out of everything if I didn't feel like doing stuff," he says. "I didn't know what I wanted to do—should I stay in Hickory [North Carolina], go into the military, or go to college?" Since he didn't have the money for college, John took the ASVAB. He racked up a perfect score.

"The recruiters were all over me—the Marines, Air Force, and Army. For a while the Air Force looked like a possibility. But the openings in the Air Force were only in administrative programs."

Things to Remember If You Become Disillusioned

➤ Enlisting in the military is a very serious matter.

➤ If you decide you don't want to stay in the military, or if you get into some sort of trouble, you will soon discover you are in a "legal process." The system is stacked against you.

➤ If you do get into trouble, insist upon your right to an attorney. If the attorney provided doesn't help you, ask to see another one. That is your right.

➤ Everything in the military requires that you sign papers. Do not sign anything just because someone tries to intimidate you. Keep careful notes of what your superior officers say and do to you.

➤ From the time you enlist in the military, you are trained to do what you are told. But when you are in trouble, the only way you will get a fair hearing is by not signing any papers that waive your rights. Yelling foul after you are released from the service will not help if you have signed papers that give up your rights.

And he turned down the Army and the Marines "because I didn't want to get yelled at." When the Navy offered him a program in identification work—in the Signal Corps—John signed on. "I was given a lot of responsibility," he says.

And John learned "a lot about taking responsibility for myself. In the Navy, everything was up to me. There was no one to rescue me, and there is no second chance in a lot of situations. I learned that I was an adult with adult responsibilities."

John also took advantage of the educational possibilities the Navy offered. In addition to putting $1,200 into the GI Bill fund (which grew to $14,000-plus upon his discharge), he started taking college courses while he was stationed in Norfolk, Virginia. Most people take only one course a semester. "I wound up going to classes four nights a week. The Navy paid for everything."

Although John was accepted into Annapolis and gave it serious consideration, just a few days before he was to be sworn in, he decided he wanted to go to a regular college. "I realized my heart wasn't in it." He felt that there was a downside to a long-term commitment to the military. "In the military, creativity isn't stressed. If you fulfill your job, you'll go far. But no one wants your opinion. The Navy is not a college. You do what they tell you to do."

At the end of his two-year enlistment, John left the Navy and went to Appalachian State in North Carolina, where he did a double major in psychology and business. One of the things John is especially proud of is the fact that he graduated from college just after he turned 22—basically the same time most of his high school friends graduated. Today John is an assistant manager in the loan department at a major bank in Raleigh. He is planning on going on to graduate school to earn an M.B.A. "Eventually, I'd like to run my own company. I want to be challenged."

"My advice to people who are thinking of joining the service is to check out all your options. Keep an open mind. Some people won't be able to take the pressure of military life. And frankly, if they had given me the option of getting out after six months, I would have taken it. But I'm glad that I had those two years in the Navy. It's a place where I grew up."

"I learned when I can open my mouth and when I shouldn't"

One thing Max Margolis knew when he finished high school was that he hated school. "I don't know why. I just thought it was really boring." Nevertheless, he dutifully went off to college at the University of St. Louis, joined a fraternity, and "had a really good time." He didn't do very much schoolwork and managed to hang in there for a year and a half before he went back home. After trying community college for a semester, he realized that he "really didn't want to be in school at all." So Max headed back to St. Louis, where he still had some friends. He ended up working in a sub shop and a cell phone store. But after a while, things began to pall. "Even though I didn't want to be in college, I didn't like the feeling of being useless. I felt like I was wasting my time sitting around."

So Max began to think seriously about joining a branch of the military. He considered joining the Navy for quite a while, and when he noticed that the recruiting station was right across from the sub shop, he took that as a good omen. And with everyone—namely, his parents—pressuring him to decide what to do with the rest of his life, Max decided that he could at least figure out what to do over the next couple of years. He joined the Navy and signed up to train as a medic. He was interested in becoming a firefighter and knew that he'd need certification as an EMT (emergency medical technician). He also knew that if he changed his mind while he was in the Navy, he could switch jobs after two years.

Max went off to boot camp in Illinois. "Boot camp was rough, even though I expected it," he said. "It was really hard." But he is certain that so far, this is the best thing he's done with his life, and the Navy has certainly changed him.

"It's given me an appreciation for money, that's for sure. I see very little of it right now. And I had a hard time following orders. That's just something you learn, to bite your tongue. I've had problems with that a lot of times. I learned when I can open my mouth and when I shouldn't. I learned to respect people who are in the military, and I've learned to respect people who have hard jobs all day long."

And Max stopped being messy. "You take me at college, in a fraternity, a messy guy, washing my clothes maybe once every month and a half, wearing wrinkled shirts and everything. Now I feel weird going out of my room with wrinkled pants, so I iron everything before I go out. My civilian boots used to be scuffed. Now everything is polished. Things that never even crossed my mind before, I do now."

The Navy has given Max a sense of purpose, something to work for, and he has a life to look forward to. "And you know, I'm thinking that I'll probably wind up going back to school after the military. If I'd just gone to school, it would have cut out a lot of hardships." Before, he had all of his bills, as well as his college tuition paid by his parents. "Now I have to earn it. Now I'm responsible for myself." Max has signed up to serve for five years in the Navy. By the time he gets out, he will have $40,000 waiting for his college education. And while he's onboard his ship, he's been taking college courses online, paid for by the U.S. Navy. Instead of feeling useless, he's already taken part in several rescue missions, including actually saving a fellow seaman's life.

"I feel that most people who make something out of their lives," says Max, "have had to work hard for it."

"The army was my escape route"

Curtis Letterlough joined the army at 17. "I was still in high school," Curtis says. "The Army has a special program called a 'split option'—I was able to enlist while still in high school and start the first part of my enlistment by going to basic training, and then come back and complete my senior year in high school." This program, which is open to high school students, actually places high school students in the Reserves. Once a month during his senior year, Curtis had to report for a weekend of Reserve training. He also received a stipend, which currently is $172 a month.

After Curtis graduated from high school, he finished his training as a truck driver. He learned to drive and repair multi-axle vehicles. Currently, he's part of a ground ambulance unit that saw action in Iraq.

Curtis, who is African American, grew up in the projects in Baltimore, Maryland. "You know, growing up in the city of Baltimore, a lot of people my age were into drugs. That wasn't a part of me. I was always looking for something better to do. Going into the Army gave me the chance to do something different and better. The Army was my escape route."

Curtis gave a lot of credit to a middle school teacher who had hall duty for setting him straight. He kept getting kicked out of class for being disruptive, and the teacher was able to establish a special bond with Curtis. Later, Curtis met the teacher's wife, and the relationship blossomed into a deep friendship with both of them.

"I grew up in a home where my mother was always getting high, folks there were all getting high, and I didn't have anyone stable that I could count on and be there for me"—except for this teacher and his wife. Curtis felt he could always come over to their house and sit down and talk to them. "They would take me out to McDonald's and talk. And there was something special about sitting down to a meal and eating with them. They were always there for me. I was basically out there on my own. You know, a lot of people who grow up in the city, they can't see why things are like that. I had something special."

Curtis is the first person in four generations of his family to graduate from high school. And he's the only one in his family who has been able to maintain a career in the military.

The four months Curtis spent in Iraq were emotionally difficult. His job with the ground ambulance unit was to respond quickly when someone was injured. He became a "combat life saver," in addition to his main job as a basic marksman and mechanic. While in Iraq he had to learn how to do basic first aid and administer an intravenous feed. "The hardest thing," he said, "was to see children who were hurt and couldn't be saved." Also, as a mechanic, "we had to pull over and fix a vehicle right on the spot, despite what was happening. We had to get the job done even under fire. We had a few incidents where people fired at us, and our people got hit.

Curtis Letterlough in uniform (Curtis Letterlough)

"Being in a Third World country and seeing the poverty level and seeing how things were a lot different from where I came from, and not knowing whom to trust—except the people who are the U.S. forces—well, your stress level goes up a lot. I was cautious, and a lot of times I was scared."

Still, Curtis sees the Army as "a good thing. It will take care of you. You have so many opportunities to do things you never thought you could do and become someone you never thought you would be. It takes an understanding that everyone has a place. Once you find it, you can maintain it. Discipline is a main factor. You learn to hunker down and be respectful. It's stressful being a black man, especially in Baltimore. But being in uniform, I stand out. You will not get harassed, and you won't catch the eye of the police, and you get more respect. People aren't so quick to judge you when you're in uniform."

Although Curtis started out as a devil-may-care fun-loving 17-year-old, today, at 21, he has become a responsible adult. "You learn that things may not be fair, things happen that are out of your control, but you have to be a man or woman enough to say, 'Well, this is what happened, and this is how I contributed to it, whether it be right or wrong. And this is how I'm going to deal with it.' You take things as they come."

A FINAL NOTE

One of the most striking things about the people in this chapter is how good they felt about what they accomplished while they served their country. Clearly, those who were most successful were those who thought carefully about themselves and had at least one specific goal in mind. Even Tim Ryan, who became disillusioned after completing only half of his hitch, came out of the experience with very positive feelings about the Air Force and what it did for him. John Weeldreyer was a very different person from when he

The Current Deal

There have been a number of changes to military contracts over the years. Sergeant First Class Matthew J. Blair, who is station commander of the U.S. Army Recruiting Station in Ithaca, New York, says that it is no longer possible to wind up in the military without a specific job. "Today there are no more 'open contracts.' Everyone signs up for a specific job." And surprisingly, your contract will say that you are actually signing up for eight years! However, every recruit can specify whether he or she wants to be on active duty for anywhere from two to eight years, and you will be discharged after the active duty is over. Technically, you remain in the Inactive Ready Reserves for the remainder of that eight-year period, although your chances of being recalled are very small. However, in time of war, Inactive Ready Reserves are called up.

Also, the military offers some excellent financial deals, including bonuses of up to $20,000 if you sign on to do a specific job that is needed, or if you bring in another recruit. (Not all branches of the military offer the full $20,000. The Marines, for example, have a cap of $6,000, and most bonuses are less.) And even if you decide not to take the college tuition option, while you are in the military, all college courses will be paid for.

entered the service. For many young men and women who choose the military, the answer to the question posed in this chapter is a resounding yes. But for Curtis Letterlough, who saw death and destruction on an unimaginable level, there are emotional scars that will forever run deep.

Chapter VIII

Early College Admission: A Wise Choice for Smart Kids?

D O YOU FEEL YOU ARE SIMPLY WASTING TIME IN HIGH SCHOOL? Are you the sort of person who gets your homework done in 15 minutes because the assignment is so easy? Have you ever had the experience of being out of school for a long period of time only to discover you hadn't missed much? Do you feel that your senior (or junior or even sophomore) year of high school is going to be boring instead of intellectually stimulating? Do you wish, more than anything, that you could be in college right now?

Lorin Dytel was determined to graduate from high school in Jericho, New York, when she was 16. She had a difficult time convincing her school to let her do this. She was the first person from her community to be accepted into The Johns Hopkins Center for Talented Youth (CTY) summer program. She'd been going there every summer since the seventh grade and had taken so many advanced-placement courses that her high school had nothing more to offer. "I liked it at CTY," she says. "I was really academically challenged and met other kids who liked the same things I did." Knowing that college-level courses were so much more exciting compared to her high school courses convinced Lorin to complete her secondary education as soon as possible.

Of the five colleges Lorin applied to, she was accepted at two and chose to go to the University of Chicago. "I know that I didn't get into some of the other colleges because of my age, but being a younger student at Chicago doesn't really make a difference. Although," she concedes, "you might have more problems socially if you are a male. There are fewer females at Chicago, so the social life for women is great."

Of course, Lorin had to limit her social activities because of the workload. "It really shocked me," she says. "Every weekday, except for Friday nights, I studied. It took me until the second quarter to get the hang of it. But I definitely liked the great conversations we had there. It was a lot better than in high school. College is a very different kind of life from high school."

Center for Talented Youth
Institute for the Academic Advancement of Youth
Johns Hopkins University
3400 North Charles Street
Baltimore, MD 21218
(410) 516-0337
(410) 516-0804
ctyinfo@jhu.edu
http://www.cty.jhu.edu

Kimberly Carter of Edison, New Jersey, wasn't a straight-A student at her high school. "But," she says, "I love to study things that interest me." The summer after her junior year, Kimberly attended Rutgers University Summer College for high school students. "I knew even before the summer was over that I didn't want to go back to high school. I was taking this course in archaeology, and we were doing some actual digging in an ancient Leni-Lenape settlement in Washington County. It was the most exciting thing I'd ever done."

When Kimberly spoke with the summer college advisor, she discovered that Rutgers offered an early-admission option. She instantly applied. Even though Kimberly's high school grades included a couple of Cs, recommendations from her summer college professors were very strong.

"My parents were definitely not happy about this," says Kimberly. "They figured they had one more year before they'd have to help me with college costs, and I had two other siblings still in college." So she offered to live at home and commute the short distance to the New Brunswick campus to save money. Rutgers offered her enough work-study opportunities to meet the modest tuition costs her first year. "I was just happy going to college," she says. "I didn't much care if I lived on campus or not."

EXPLORING YOUR OPTIONS

Perhaps skipping one or even two years of high school and going to college early is right for you. In years past, it was an option for only a tiny minority of students, and usually a student had to prove that he or she had taken all the advanced-placement classes the high school had to offer. However, today there is a small but important revolution in public education. More and more educators have come to recognize that motivated students can complete the first two years of high school and the first two years of college in the time it takes to complete the traditional four years of high school. Partnerships between public education and colleges and universities are beginning to emerge so that qualified students can complete two years of college absolutely free.

The pioneer in this field is the Bard High School Early College in partnership with the New York City Department of Education. In 2001, Bard College collaborated with New York City to offer 260 motivated students an unusual opportunity. By enrolling in the Bard High School Early College, they completed their high school requirements in just two years. Years three and four were spent taking a rigorous college program with an emphasis on writing and the arts and humanities. Graduates of the Bard High

School Early College (the first class graduated in June 2003) received not only a Regents high school diploma, but also an A.A. (associate of arts) degree from Bard, a small, innovative private college.

Graduates of the program then transfer their credits to a four-year college. Today there are 500 students at the Bard High School Early College, and more than 4,000 students apply for the 140 spaces available in each incoming class.

This program has proved so successful that others are trying to replicate it in several large cities across the United States. The funding for the newest early college public schools in partnership with various colleges has come from several sources, including the Bill and Melinda Gates Foundation, the Carnegie Corporation of New York, the Ford Foundation, and the W.K. Kellogg Foundation. The goal is to create 70 early college high schools in various sites nationwide by 2007. Some of these partnerships will be in large cities in Ohio, California, New York, and Oregon. Others will serve rural areas in Utah and other sparsely populated states. Some of these schools will focus on minority students, while others will be open to all students in a given area.

To find out if there is an early college high school in your area, go to http://www.earlycolleges.org/partners.html

To find out more about the Bard High School Early College, e-mail bhsec@bard.edu, or phone (212) 995-8479.

Figuring out what's right for you

Getting into college early isn't easy. For one thing, many high schools don't like losing their top students, and some colleges don't really like the idea of accepting younger students. But such roadblocks should not stop you if you are serious about going to college before you finish four years of high school.

Dr. Julian C. Stanley, who pioneered the program for academically talented youth in the 1970s at Johns Hopkins University, notes that while there are many colleges, including Hopkins, that accept younger students, most don't provide any special supports for them. It can be difficult for a 15- or 16-year-old living in a college dorm to adjust to the kind of college life a typical 18-year-old student lives. "Often," Dr. Stanley says, "the younger student who commutes to college has an easier time."

An independent learner

Emily Goldman, who was formally admitted to Cornell University when she was 16, found this to be true. Even though she had been taking college courses since she was 14 at both Ithaca College and Cornell (where her mother taught in the business school), living on campus that first semester as a full-time student proved challenging. Technically, Emily was home-schooled off and on between seventh grade and high school. But

Violinist Jina Lee, pianist Emily Goldman, and cellist Sara Rice (from left) form a trio. (Kathy Morris)

in fact, she was rarely home. An independent and highly motivated learner, Emily pursued her own interests, reading in a wide variety of disciplines. She was also a serious piano student, took music courses at Ithaca College, and performed before audiences both as a soloist and in chamber ensembles from the time she was eleven years old. After focusing on literature and music for two years as an extramural student, Emily decided she was ready to go to college full time.

"The fact that I had [college] transcripts and grades helped a lot," she said. She wasn't required to take the New York State Regents exams, but she did have to prepare a portfolio of the things she'd done outside of the courses she'd taken.

Emily also won a special scholarship to the Telluride Program, a self-governing cooperative run by students who live and eat together. It is a very competitive program, and she had to submit an essay and be screened by those already living in the house. There are special events, special lectures given by professors just for Telluride residents, and much more. Emily was the youngest person there, one of only two freshmen, and "socially," she says, "it's a real pressure cooker. It's an exciting and intellectual commune, and while you are in the system, it takes many hours of your time."

For someone like Emily, who had spent several years "not isolated, but leading a pretty solitary existence," the experience proved overwhelming. At first she tried to treat her "social and living situation somewhat like another college course." But it became clear to her that the pressure she put on herself to succeed there was "over the top." It was beginning to affect her health. So, after the first semester, she decided "it was a good idea to go back home, take my classes, and step back." This gave her a chance to think about what she really wanted from her college experience. By the beginning of her sophomore year, Emily felt confident enough to go back on campus and live in one of the regular dorms with friends. She has the option of returning to Telluride at any time during her college years.

Since music has always been an important part of her life, Emily thought through what she loved most and what she hated most about the music scene. "The thing I dread most is performing solo concerts. But performing in ensembles, especially chamber music, is something I love." As a result of this understanding, Emily has begun to enjoy music in a new way. "I'm starting to write music, and this past year I took a course in conducting." She is pursuing a double major in music and literature and is now a happy college student about to enter her junior year.

A step-by-step approach

Leela Steiner used her community college as a jumping-off place once she decided not to continue on in high school. She had gone to alternative public schools in Ithaca, New York, from the time she was in the second grade. Her sophomore year of high school was spent in an alternative school in Teaneck, New Jersey. When she returned to Ithaca the following year, she didn't want to go to either the traditional or alternative high school. "I had already taken a couple of courses at Fairleigh Dickinson University. I'd taken advanced-placement summer courses at Smith College, and I thought I could handle college," she says.

Leela was two months short of 16 when she enrolled in Tompkins Cortland Community College in Dryden, New York. She had decided on the community college route because she hadn't taken the SATs, which most community colleges don't require.

Happily, she found several other high school "dropouts" enrolled at the college that semester, and the four became close friends. But by the end of the first semester, she found the academics less challenging than she'd hoped. Nevertheless, it was time well spent. "The community college got me into the semester system and into taking finals."

She transferred to Ithaca College, which accepted her community college courses and didn't require that she take the SATs since she'd already proved she could do college work. At Ithaca College, Leela discovered the courses were extremely rigorous. "I had very hard classes at Ithaca College, because my dad [who was a professor there] had recommended the most high-powered teachers to me. I got into college before there were lots of requirements, but it turned out that because I was curious about things, I took a lot of what was later required."

But what if you don't want to be thrown into a sink-or-swim situation with all the other older college students? Well, there are a small but growing number of colleges that do have special programs especially designed for the early college student. Three are private colleges. Others are public colleges, some of which are open only to in-state students. Others are open to all who qualify.

PRIVATE COLLEGES

Simon's Rock College of Bard

Simon's Rock College of Bard, located in Great Barrington, Massachusetts, was founded in 1968. It has a total student body of 350 and is the only liberal-arts college in the United States designed solely for the early college student. Its entire freshman class is composed of students between the ages of 14 and 16. Students who complete the first two years are awarded an Associate of Arts degree. At that point they either transfer to another four-year college or reapply to comp͏ ͏͏ degree at Simon's Rock.

Vice president and dean of the college Bernᵢ is important not to "simply admit students iͳ they are a minority, without providing special feel the best way to serve these young stud educate them among their peers. An adolescent who is intellectually capable of doing college work is still an adolescent emotionally. At Simon's Rock, close attention is paid to the student's life outside the class. There are many more services available to Simon's Rock students than at traditional colleges, as well as a higher ratio of adult resident counselors."

Recently Simon's Rock has begun a national talent search aimed at tenth graders whose "achievements merit the opportunity to attend Simon's Rock with a full scholarship." At the present time there are 30 full scholarships awarded each year under the Acceleration to Excellence fund. Tuition with room and board is currently $36,580. There are numerous partial and full scholarships available.

PEG at Mary Baldwin College

In 1984, the all-women's Mary Baldwin College in Staunton, Virginia, established PEG (Program for the Exceptionally Gifted). Students who are accepted into the program must have completed at least eighth grade. For the first two years the girls live in separate dormitories with resident counselors who provide a lot of support. There are programs tailored to the special emotional and social needs of young college students. All college courses are taken with the traditional Mary Baldwin students. Tuition and fees for the PEG program are $24,939. Approximately 99 percent of the students receive financial assistance.

The Clarkson School

The Clarkson School was founded in 1971 specifically for talented young people interested in the sciences. It offers a special one-year "bridge" program to students who have finished eleventh ~~de~~ (and other grades, in special cases) and are truly ready for ~~llenge~~ of college work.

Gary F. Kelly, headmaster at Clarkson, says, "We seek students who have done well in their present setting and who have scored high on the SATs. Our average math score is 700 [out of a possible 800]. Average verbal score is 600. In addition, we look for the accelerated high school student who has been recommended by the people who know the student best." Clarkson students have taken all the advanced-placement courses offered by their high schools and have enhanced their studies at such places as The Johns Hopkins Center for Talented Youth, Northwestern University, Duke University, and the University of North Carolina.

The 70 to 100 or so students admitted to The Clarkson School take their classes with the regular Clarkson University students. However, they live in separate housing apart from the other students. ("Actually," says one "schoolie," "our housing is much better than freshman housing.") Each house accommodates eight to ten students, plus a resident counselor. All take part in once-a-week "family style" dinners with Clarkson faculty and staff and get to go on special trips. Most Clarkson School students transfer to other universities after their "bridge" year, although a few opt to continue at Clarkson University. Tuition with room, board, and other fees at The Clarkson School is $36,890. The average scholarship is $7,525, but scholarships range from $1,000 all the way up to $17,000.

Simon's Rock College of Bard
84 Alford Road
Great Barrington, MA 01230-9702
Mary King Austin, Director of Admission
(800) 235-7186
admit@simons-rock.edu
http://www.simons-rock.edu

PEG at Mary Baldwin College
Staunton, VA 24401
Jill Urquhart, Director of Admission
(540) 887-7039
(540) 887-7187
peg@mbc.edu
http://www.mbc.edu/peg

The Clarkson School
Clarkson University
Chad Tessier, Director of Admission
P.O. Box 5650
Potsdam, NY 13699-5650
(800) 574-4425
tcs@clarkson.edu
http://www.clarkson.edu/~tcs

STATE-SUPPORTED SCHOOLS

A handful of states have recognized the need to encourage their brightest students, especially those from communities where there are limited educational resources. Texas has instituted two early college options. The program at Lamar University in Beaumont, Texas, known as Texas Academy of Leadership in the Humanities (TALH), began in 1993 and has grown from just 35 students the first year to 150 now. The Texas Academy of Mathematics and Science (TAMS) at the University of North Texas in Denton has been accepting students since 1987 and admits 200 students each year. Both TAMS and TALH are open only to residents of Texas, and both are two-year programs. The TALH program emphasizes development of leadership skills and liberal arts. The TAMS program focuses primarily on math and science. Students at TAMS pay $3,050 for room and board. Tuition, books, and lab fees are free. Tuition, room, and board at TALH is $5,300. Scholarships are

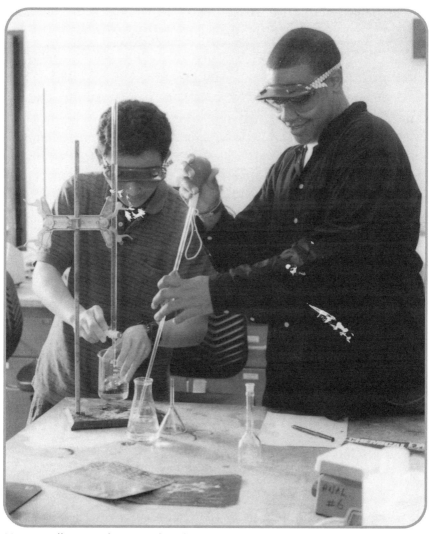

Young college students get hands-on experience in a chemistry lab at the Advanced Academy of Georgia at the State University of West Georgia. (Advanced Academy of Georgia)

available. Both programs recruit students who have completed tenth grade.

In 1995, the state of Georgia chartered the Advanced Academy of Georgia at the State University of West Georgia located in Carrollton, about 50 miles outside of Atlanta. This program, which began with just 21 students, will expand as the need increases. Unlike the Texas programs, it is open to both in-state and out-of-state students who have completed the tenth or eleventh grades. Room, board, and other student fees for Georgia residents are approximately $7,000. They pay no tuition. Out-of-state students pay approximately $14,000.

The state of Georgia has also chartered the Georgia Academy of Mathematics, Engineering & Science (GAMES) at Middle Georgia College, located in Cochran, Georgia. GAMES has been designed to meet the needs of gifted high school juniors and seniors who have exceptional ability and interest in engineering, mathematics, science, computers, and allied health fields. And GAMES, like the Advanced Academy of Georgia, is open to both in-state and out-of-state students. The program had 50 students for the 1998–99 school year. The annual cost for GAMES is $5,000 for Georgia residents; out-of-state students pay approximately $8,500 per year. Financial aid is available.

There are stiff entrance requirements for each of these state-funded early college programs.

The Advanced Academy of Georgia
Honors House
The State University of West Georgia
Carrollton, GA 30118
(770) 836-4449
afinch@westga.edu
http://www.westga.edu/~academy

The Georgia Academy of Math, Engineering & Science (GAMES)
Middle Georgia College
1100 Second Street, SE
Cochran, GA 31014
(478) 934-3471
games@warrior.mgc.peachnet.edu
http://www.mgc.peachnet.edu

Texas Academy of Mathematics and Science (TAMS)
University of North Texas
P.O. Box 305309
Denton, TX 76203-5309
(800) 241-TAMS
admissions@tams.unt.edu
http://www.tams.unt.edu

Texas Academy of Leadership in the Humanities (TALH)
Lamar University
P.O. Box 10062
Beaumont, TX 77710-0062
(409) 839-2995
(409) 839-2991
talh@hal.lamar.edu
http://hal.lamar.edu/~talh

There are a sprinkling of other commuter-based programs throughout the country. Among these are the Program at California State University in Los Angeles, which accepts students who are at least 11 years old but not older than 15 and a half, and the Early Entrance Program at the University of Washington in Seattle, Washington, which accepts students under the age of 15.

Early Entrance Program
California State University at Los Angeles
5151 State University Drive
Los Angeles, CA 90032-8530
(323) 343-3000
admission@calstatela.edu
http://www.calstatela.edu

Halbert and Nancy Robinson Center for Young Scholars
University of Washington
P.O. Box 351630
Seattle, WA 98195-1630
(206) 543-4160
(206) 685-3890
cscy@u.washington.edu.
http://depts.washington.edu/cscy

WHO GOES TO COLLEGE EARLY AND WHY

Students go to college early for a variety of reasons. Not all of them are sound ones. So it's important to take a close look at your real motives before you decide to opt out of high school. Go back to your self-assessment test and review that picture of yourself.

As you read through the stories of those who have gone to college early, see if you share some of their goals and aspirations. Those who are successful in college have an overriding desire to learn. They are emotionally ready for the challenge and will work hard to prove that they made the right choice. Many of those who chose to leave high school early didn't have a large group of friends and therefore didn't mind striking out on their own. Others were popular with their high school classmates but were eager to accept new and difficult challenges. Says Kimberly, "Studying is a solitary activity. If you think spending five hours a night in the library is fun, then going to college early is for you. People who do well academically have to put in hours of studying by themselves. It's a natural extension of yourself."

Another student warns, "If your sole reason is to party and get away from your parents, going to college early would be a waste of your time."

People who choose to go to college early come from a variety of backgrounds. Some are from small rural high schools, where they feel totally out of sync with the rest of the students. Others have already taken college courses, either during summer vacations or as part of their high school curriculum, and feel, as Leela did, that they can handle a full college load. Some are straight-A students and have been labeled "gifted and talented" by their school districts. Others are doing rather ordinary work in high school because they haven't been challenged, but often they study subjects that interest them on their own.

Placed in the wrong high school

Rodney Christopher, an African-American student from the Crown Heights section of Brooklyn, New York, didn't make it into either of his two first-choice high schools. He did get into Brooklyn Technical High School. Many high schools in New York City have a special focus, and students have to pass exams in order to get into the better ones. Through a computer error, Rodney's application for his first choice was voided, so he decided to make the best of it at his third choice.

"I did really well there," he says, "and I didn't hate it. Yet I didn't know what I wanted to do. I just knew that this wasn't it." By the end of his sophomore year, Rodney was ranked first in his class of 1,200. He'd taken his PSATs, and shortly after his scores were out, he received a brochure from Simon's Rock College of Bard.

"The brochure was very inviting," he says. So he and his mother visited the campus. "Everyone at Simon's Rock was just so friendly," Rodney says. It was very different from what he'd been experiencing in New York. "It was actually exciting to just say hello to people you didn't know. It made me very happy, and as I was being interviewed, I felt like I was being treated as if I were older. I realized I was applying to a normal college."

Rodney received the DuBois Scholarship and became a freshman (or "freshling," as first year students are called there) at 16.

His Brooklyn friends and teachers were surprised by Rodney's decision. Even though none of them knew anything about the college, they told Rodney he was making a big mistake. They thought that getting a liberal-arts education instead of a scientific one was not a wise thing to do. "But not for me," says Rodney. "I felt there were so many things I wanted to learn that weren't available at my high school. I felt stifled." His mother was completely won over by their visit. "She knew I'd like it here."

Getting away from a place you don't like

Kim Cooper completed two of the "happiest years of my life" at TAMS. She came from the small town (population 3,500) of West (which is actually north of Waco, Texas). "It is the *kolacky* capital of the world," says Kim. (*Kolacky*, Kim explains, is a Czech specialty—a fried dough that is stuffed with meat and other things.) "My old high school had about 100 kids in my class. Our science labs were pathetic. They hadn't been updated since the 1950s. West is a town where sports is king, and the folks there keep voting to build new sports facilities. There was nothing there for me."

One of the most exciting aspects of TAMS was that "for the first time I met really intelligent students, and we didn't get the grief we had experienced in our regular high schools. Here you can be yourself. No one will pick on you because you are bright. One night a bunch of us stayed up talking about what it was like for us in our home high school—and we all found that we'd had difficulties. Most people didn't understand us. So it was important to find out that we'd all gone through some rough times. You know, most of us came here because we wanted to get away from a place we didn't like. Now that I've graduated, I can tell you that we'd do this again because of all the friends we've made."

All his friends had left

Andy Pasqual of Clarkson, Georgia, was already dissatisfied with his high school when he received a letter from the Advanced

Academy of Georgia. "We [he and his parents] had already been looking for alternatives because my school wasn't working out. I wasn't being challenged, and a lot of my friends had left. Several had moved to the next county over." When he read the letter describing the Academy, he thought, "'Wow! This looks pretty cool.' It said that the Academy was for advanced high school students and that you could live there and take courses for college credit." His visit to the campus confirmed his belief that it was the place for him. In fact, some of his teachers from his high school encouraged him to move on. Also, his voice teacher at his high school was leaving, and that was another reason for Andy's desire to leave.

"I knew there would be a trade-off," Andy says. "I was going to sacrifice my last two years of high school and I wouldn't be able to do some of my favorite high school activities anymore." One thing that especially bothered him was the National Honor Society. "I was pretty much in the running to be the next year's president, and when my sponsor found I was applying to this program, they wouldn't even let me run. I was being separated out. I didn't feel too good about that."

> "I was going to sacrifice my last two years of high school and I wouldn't be able to do some of my favorite high school activities."

There were some other trade-offs as well. For one thing, there were curfews at the Academy—11 P.M. on weekdays, 12 P.M. on weekends. Students are not allowed to do varsity sports, nor can they join a sorority or fraternity—except for a service fraternity.

Anyone found drinking alcohol or using drugs is automatically dismissed from the program. These restrictions didn't bother Andy. In fact, to him "the Academy seemed like this extra-long summer camp, only you had to study.

"I had a great time at West Georgia. I was so challenged. It was," he admits, "a lot harder than I thought. I got involved in a lot of things. I joined the Chamber Singers [the college chorus]. And it was the first time they had had high school kids in their chorus."

> "I had a great time at West Georgia. I was so challenged. I got involved in a lot of things."

Andy also liked the fact that the regular college students and the professors didn't know who the Academy students were unless the student told someone. "People assumed I was a college student." And when people did find out, "most thought it was pretty cool. But other students had a different experience. Some professors did resent the fact that high school kids were in their classes."

Andy learned that it was important to keep in touch with his home school. "Otherwise you can lose out on scholarship and other financial aid that may be available to you as a high school student." He also thought it might be a good idea for early college students to "have in mind the college they want to go to when they finish the early college part. This is because some four-year colleges won't accept early college credits from the Academy." If that happens, you will have to begin your four-year college as a freshman.

Andy chose Furman University in South Carolina when he had completed the two years at the Academy. Furman accepted virtually all 62 credits, allowing him to enter with junior standing. However, Andy intends to stay at Furman for four years because

kids in the program, and that her French was the worst. "I was freaked out by that." But "the one thing I have is pride, and to go home and go back to school after I'd made this huge deal about being the first exchange student from my high school—if nothing else, pride will do a lot to keep a person from giving up."

After a three-week session at a language institute in the city of Tours, Laura and one other student were placed with families in Colmar, close to the German border. Laura didn't always enjoy her living situation because the host family didn't make their rules clear at the outset. For example, her family used the telephone only for quick messages, not for long chats with friends. And unlike phone companies in most cities in the U.S., which don't charge for local calls, all phone calls in France are charged by the minute. Of course, once she understood the problem, Laura used a phone card and called her friends from a pay phone, but the damage to their relationship was already done. In hindsight, Laura says, it would have been better if she had been more proactive by asking questions first.

However, going to the local high school turned out to be exciting in several different ways. French students are very serious about their studies, and Laura "learned what it meant to be a serious student. The senior year in a French high school is very intense. It's like going to college."

Two important things happened while she was there. The first of these was a "huge student strike. It was the biggest student strike since 1968—and it was over the fact that the minister of education wanted to charge tuition in the colleges, which had always been free." The strike soon spread to Belgium and Germany. "It was really amazing. The students actually closed the schools for three weeks and we marched around the town and sat in the middle of intersections—that's when I really bonded with the other students. The strike was totally organized by the high school students. They were saying, 'We won't accept that. And we have power.'

"And the second thing that happened was, just before I left they threw this huge celebration party in my honor. People brought me presents. People wrote cards and they did things which totally made me cry. They remembered when I first came, and we talked about stereotypes—the ones I held about the French and those they held about Americans (reruns of *Dallas* were big, and they all wanted to know if I had an oil well in my backyard). They remembered that I said I thought that there would be French men waiting for me at the airport who would drink champagne from my shoe, write me beautiful poems, and send me flowers. Well, two boys in the class wrote me poems and they read them to the entire class. It was so funny and sweet."

While Laura was in France, she kept in close touch with her mother, who kept track of when applications to colleges were due. She was accepted at several colleges and decided on New York University. Laura was now confident that she could handle the challenge of both New York City and a tough university program.

The Experiment in International Living
P.O. Box 595
63 Main Street
Brattleboro, VT 05346
(802) 387-4210
(802) 387-5783 (fax)
federation@experiment.org
http://www.experiment.org
Note: EIL now offers only summer abroad programs in 19 different countries for high school students.

A COMMITMENT TO PEACE AND INTERNATIONAL UNDERSTANDING

By the time Amity Weiss had finished her junior year of high school, she was tired of the environment there. "I wanted something more than my high school had to offer. I didn't dislike my school. It was a very good one. I was just tired of the social atmosphere, and I wanted to leave home, and I wanted an international experience."

Amity had racked up a number of successes over the years, including winning a $10,000 college scholarship from *Seventeen* magazine when she was in the sixth grade for her social activism. She had created an organization of her peers called KidsReach, which studied trouble spots in the world and then found ways to raise money to help children in war-torn countries. Her most successful project was getting her entire school to make a video and send letters and money to buy school supplies for children in the city of Bihac in Bosnia. The group continued to engage in international study and activism throughout their high school years.

Amity learned about the United World Colleges through her Canadian aunt, who lived near a United World College there. There are 11 schools throughout the world, in Hong Kong, India, Italy, Norway, Singapore, Swaziland, the United Kingdon, the United States, Venezuela, and Wales. Around 1,000 students from 80 countries are chosen to attend the two-year programs, which focus on community service and cultural and outdoor activities, as well as a commitment to peace and international understanding. Students complete their senior year of high school and their freshman year of college in a variety of disciplines. They live a very intense multicultural life, and everyone who is chosen for the program receives full scholarships, including airfare for those from poorer countries. "This program isn't just for rich kids. Although perhaps 10 percent of the kids are very wealthy, 20 percent are from poorer countries, and the rest of us are considered middle class in our own countries. We all come from very diverse backgrounds."

Once she was accepted into United World Colleges, Amity could choose where she wanted to study. She chose Italy because it was close to the Balkans, an area she had studied and visited. "The main problem, no matter where you go, however, is culture shock. It wasn't as bad for me, because I'd spent time in a lot of different countries. But European culture took getting used to." Although all classes for all the programs are in English, and Amity was fluent in Spanish, there were many different languages being spoken at any one time. "My Italian definitely got better," she said, and she picked up a sprinkling of other languages.

The school was in northern Italy, in a little town called Duino. "We lived in the old servants' quarters of a large castle." She had roommates from Argentina and Israel. Classes began at 8 A.M., and she was required to take courses in English, Italian, a science, humanities, and math. For electives, Amity chose art history and European history. As her community service experience project, she also took on volunteering in a refugee camp in nearby Slovenia four afternoons a week. This proved to be a stressful but very rewarding experience. She worked not only with children, but also with some elderly people who had been living in the camp for eight or nine years. "And," she says, she observed "a lot of rackets going on." Some of the medication meant for the refugees was being skimmed by one of the people running the camp and sold to stores outside.

Besides community service, all the students engaged in a variety of sports activities. Soccer was popular, "but if you didn't want to do sports, you didn't really have to." Amity did basketball and jogging and started a girls' hockey team. There was also an excellent photography program and a place where students could learn mediation skills. "If you had an idea that you wanted to do something, people were receptive. I did pottery and worked on a play. One kid created a computer program to teach English to our students who didn't speak it too well. And I did programs on how to study for the SATs." Many students from outside the United States were anxious to study at an American college.

Amity did have some problems. "I was a bit too social my first year. My academics and my sanity suffered. I was trying to be friends with everyone, and it took me a while to figure out who I wanted my friends to be. Also, I got into the program because of my activism background. I wasn't the valedictorian or anything. But kids who come from Hungary, for example, are winners of a difficult math competition. They are the best in their country. I wasn't the best. The kids from the U.S., Canada, and South America are generally well-rounded people, not necessarily the best. Most people have to learn to balance the social life and school work. It took me a whole year to get the hang of it. And I was never going to be a studying wonk." In her second year, however, Amity lived up to her academic potential—and was accepted at Princeton, where she has now completed her freshman year. If she had gotten all As she could have been accepted to Princeton as a sophomore. "But what was important to me," she says, "were the friendships and not the academics. You get a feel for something beyond culture. You learn how people think about things in a different way, and you begin to see things from a lot of different perspectives. There is such a diversity of opinion," she says.

"This program is not for everyone. If it is something you will like, you will know it from the interview, and as soon as you look at the material, you'll know. Trust the people interviewing you; they will know if you can make it. And it's a good idea to talk to others who have been in the program."

It's important to really know yourself. "You will question who you are many times over the two years you are there. We had world-class piano players, we had people who spoke five languages, phenomenal violin players, world-class students—so you have to have faith in yourself. It's a place where you will learn that you are not the best. There is always someone who is better than you. You need to know what you want and what you can do. Even the top pianist worried about not being the best. Everyone develops his or her own best."

A major difficulty was "being American. Even after September 11, things were difficult. Being an American is difficult these days. You are an example for your country. The anti-Americanism can be very quiet. Being open and interested is being American. In some cultures it is considered being shallow. You learn how to be an adult and not to give away too much of yourself, and how to talk to different people. I came away with a much different view of the world."

To find out more about United World Colleges, check out http://www.uwc.org.

EARLY COLLEGE IS NOT A PICNIC

Just because you have left a place you didn't like and are now a college student, it doesn't mean your problems are over. Many students worried they'd flunk out. Others were concerned about making friends. And almost all were shocked at how much time it took to study.

Rodney was afraid that "I was no longer going to do as well as I'd been doing, and that everyone was going to be smarter than me. And I was afraid people wouldn't be interested in the things I was." He was also afraid that "people were going to realize that I was poor, and that would matter."

Most of his fears were unfounded. Twenty-one percent of the students in his freshman class at Simon's Rock were minority students. "Sometimes I feel I'm in a sea of white faces, and other times it doesn't matter. Sometimes I have to adapt to what they want to do, although it is difficult to get [white kids] to adapt to what I want to do."

OVERCOMING PROBLEMS

Just as Rodney found some of the white students had notions about African Americans, he has also learned to confront his own stereotypes since he's been at Simon's Rock. "I didn't know that everyone has something worthwhile to say. I thought only those people with money, only those people who had some position of power, were worth listening to. I know better now." Even though we each come to college from vastly different backgrounds, the shared experience of college is an important basis for friendship."

Many of Leela's problems stemmed from her "quirky" alternative school education. "I almost flunked out during my first semester at Ithaca College. I didn't have the standard background, and I couldn't always understand what the professor wanted. In one class I had a D- at midterm. But by the end of the semester I had a B because the professor talked to me. I'd completely misunderstood how to write a paper." But by her sophomore year, she'd gotten so skilled at writing papers that she was offered a job in the writing lab helping less able students. In her junior year she declared a major in philosophy. "I wanted to learn logical thinking. I felt the discipline that could help me most was one that would teach me to think and reason and write logical papers. Thinking and reasoning—with those two skills I could go on to anything." Not surprisingly, the career Leela chose was law. Today she is an assistant attorney general for the state of Texas.

Kim Cooper admits her first year was tough. "It took me an entire year to learn how to study. You will have to study seven hours for exams and do at least two hours a night of homework

> **"You will have to study seven hours for exams and do at least two hours a night of homework for each course."**

for each course. But the great thing is that at TAMS you have a lot of people to study with. Yet all of the togetherness can also present problems. If you have an argument with someone, you will have to see that person every day. Living together forces you to work things out. And dating couples have problems when they break up. The thing is, you can't hide from your problems here. You have to find people to help you."

Kathleen Harpenau, who is in her second year at the TALH program at Lamar University, says that some students who come to TALH aren't responsible. "They don't go to classes, and when they find out that there is no one here to bail them out, and no mother to tell you to get up and go to class, they will fail. In this place, the more you put into it, the more you'll get out."

Sometimes students who attend the early college programs feel hemmed in when restrictions are placed on their social lives. TAMS, TALH, PEG at Mary Baldwin, The Clarkson School, and the Advanced Academy of Georgia, for example, have curfews and special programs just for the younger students. While many students feel the rules are quite liberal—more liberal than they were at home—others feel there shouldn't be restrictions on their time.

Shawn Mattot and his brother, Scott, both were accepted at The Clarkson School in different years. Neither liked the close-knit atmosphere that is consciously fostered there. Scott says, "They do crazy things at Clarkson. They want all the students to feel like a family. Now, the dorms are great. We lived in four-person suites. However, we were discouraged from meeting the regular freshmen. But the freshmen are really nice." Shawn also felt uncomfortable with the "family" environment. "I didn't care for the family atmosphere. I didn't adjust to that very well. They try to get you all to be friends. But my cousin was going to Clarkson, so I hung out with him and his friends."

Other students love the family atmosphere at their colleges. Kathleen Harpenau says, "At TALH there are 100 other students here like me. We have family groups and we discuss our problems and bond with each other. Basically, we get to know a bigger family of 100 people."

COLLEGE COURSES ARE REAL WORK— THEY MAKE YOU THINK

Virtually all of the students reported that their college courses were harder than anything else they'd undertaken. At the same time, they said the challenge was exhilarating. Moreover, many students expressed relief to be out of a place where they didn't want to be and in an atmosphere where they were valued for their intellectual abilities.

Some Tips for Parents

➣ Don't worry about the "pedigree" of the college. Worry about whether your kids are intellectually alive.

➣ Remember that most highly motivated kids are really finished with the normal high school curriculum halfway through eleventh grade.

➣ Visit with your child at the college he or she is interested in attending.

➣ Talk to other parents whose children have gone to college before completing high school. Get a variety of opinions from parents, guidance counselors, college administrators, and students—especially students.

➣ Most of all, be sensitive to the needs of your son or daughter.

"My experience here has been wonderful. For two years I've been living with all my best friends," says Kim.

"In my experience, it is the best thing that ever happened in my life," says Kathleen.

"You really did have to work, and you really did have to think," says Lorin, who received her bachelor's degree at the University of Chicago by the time she was 20 and went on to earn a master's degree. At 25, Lorin is a vice president in charge of corporate investments for a large bank in Cleveland, Ohio.

called Students of the World. When she finally returne
Kiran didn't want to attend any of the colleges in her home state.
She was still on an adventure kick. So she applied to colleges in
places that sounded exotic. "I boiled it down to three: the
University of Colorado, the University of Hawaii, and the
University of Maine. I was only looking at colleges for where they
were located. I figured that if I were going to other places in the
world, I kind of wanted to see what it was like in our country. I'd
lived in the South all of my life, and Maine seemed like a place far
away from everything. So I chose Maine."

Kiran arrived on campus full of hope and eager to make new
friends. "Because of the New Zealand and China experience,
where we were thrown into situations and had to rely on each
other, I was able to form strong friendships quickly. I was kind of
expecting the same thing when I came to Maine," she says. "I
found that not everyone was anxious to make new friends and
work together. So it was really hard." Kiran also discovered that
there were many required courses before she'd be able to take the
ones she wanted.

Even before the first semester was over, Kiran applied to a small
college not too far from her hometown, one where she was able to
plan out her own major. Despite her disappointment with her first
college choice, Kiran says, "I turned that frustration into an
understanding that I was asking too much of too big a place. I
learned a lot about Maine, and I've learned a lot on my own. I'm
able to think more clearly about my needs and my life's direction."
Kiran has since decided on a career in medicine and is pursuing
that profession.

If you and your college are a mismatch, don't throw in the towel
after a couple of uninspired weeks. What you need to do is figure
out why you and your college aren't in sync. Did you have unre-
alistic expectations? Is it the institution itself? Are the students
not interested in the same kinds of things you are? Have you

reconsidered your major interests? Once you get a handle on the problem, you can take steps to correct it. Do keep one important thing in mind: You can't change the way things are done at a college all by yourself, and you can't change the mind-set of the other students. The only thing you can change is yourself—and that involves a change of attitude.

On the other hand, perhaps you have taken stock of yourself, your grades, or your finances and decided to attend a less expensive college before heading off to the one from which you intend

Transferring Is One Way to Graduate from a More Demanding College

1. If you weren't an outstanding student while in high school, or your SAT scores were just average but you know in your heart of hearts that you are really motivated to do better, enroll in a community college for your first year and show what you can really do. With excellent grades at a community college, you will be able to transfer to a more challenging college. By then no one will be concerned with your earlier lackluster grades.

2. Colleges often look for transfer students with specific skills or majors. Transfer students fill a different need within a school. A college may be looking for a tuba player or the captain of the chess team, or it may want more students to major in French.

3. Many colleges look for students who are willing to enter in January (or March, for those on a quarter system). This is because there are always freshmen dropping out after the first semester.

4. If you can show that you've done something unusual or interesting during the semester you didn't go to college, you may be very attractive to the admissions committee.

to graduate. This can be a very wise decision. While the first college you attend may not be your dream place, you are at least grounded in why you are there, even though you are pretty certain that you will transfer after a year or two.

THINK IT THROUGH

The best way to think about choosing a college is to look at who you are and what kind of an atmosphere you'd like to be in. Don't get drawn in by the latest fad in colleges. No kidding! Colleges are subject to fads among certain groups of juniors and seniors. For several years Brown University will be hot. Another year it will be Reed College. Of course, both of these are excellent schools—but there are literally thousands of fine colleges that are not on the "hot button" list but may be just the place for you. Since you are probably a pretty independent person, you should be more interested in finding the school that suits your needs than in impressing the neighbors with a "brand name" college. Sure, a degree from one of the Ivies will impress a lot of people, including your first future employer, more than a diploma from What's-it U, but how well you do in the adult working world still depends on how well you use your own innate gifts. Don't be afraid to look into some off-the-beaten-path colleges.

If you are someone who stopped out for a while, you've already figured out that your education is really in your own hands. Your mind isn't a sausage casing into which some wise old professor will stuff her or his lifelong learning. You yourself will bring to your college experience the desire to learn, and much of what you accomplish will be because you've thought about your unique qualities during the break from schools.

Those of you choosing the early college option must pick your college with great care. Besides being open to a lesser-known school, you need to pay close attention to the social aspects of the college you choose. The social environment into which you are going has to be just right. It can't be a college that is going to just promote the intellect. It also should enhance your personal growth. Whether an early collegegoer, a late one, or right on the mark, you want to make the most informed choice you can.

Larry Colman of Winnetka, Illinois, was an early admission student at the University of Chicago, which has a long history of encouraging younger students. He had, like Lorin Dytel, just turned 16, and was tremendously excited about going there. "I'd gone for a campus visit," he says, "during one of those weekends the university sets up for prospective students. It was such a great experience. I met dozens of kids who shared my interests, and I spent hours involved in amazing discussions. I was absolutely convinced that this was the place for me."

> "I met dozens of kids who shared my interests."

By the end of the first semester, Larry had serious doubts about continuing at Chicago. "I could deal with the workload, even though it was sometimes staggering. What was so hard for me was that I had so little social life. Freshmen women weren't interested in dating freshmen guys—especially guys who are younger than they are." And remember what Lorin said—there are many more guys than gals at Chicago. Says Larry: "I just didn't know where to meet girls my own age."

Larry decided to take time out after he completed his first year—and actually found that despite his unhappiness with the social scene, "I really did quite a bit of growing up." A year later, he was ready to go back. "After all," he says, "now I'm an upper-classman. And freshmen women don't think of me as a kid."

College Tuition: More or Less

In the blink of an eye, tuition and other expenses rise at both two- and four-year colleges. According to the American Council on Education, the most recent average costs (for the academic year 2001–2002) were as follows:

➤ Two-year public colleges: tuition alone was $1,738. Add another $8,630 for living expenses.

➤ Public four-year college: tuition alone was $3,754. Add another $9,000 for living expenses. This is for in-state students. Out of state students can expect to pay $17,740 on average.

➤ Private four-year colleges and universities: tuition alone was $17,123. Add another $10,000 for living expenses.
Note: Seven out of ten students receive financial aid.

SOME QUESTIONS TO THINK ABOUT

1. Am I ready for college now? (If your answer is no, decide just how firm that no is. Some people aren't ready for college until they set foot on campus.)

2. Do I want to live at home and attend college, or is living on a college campus a priority?

3. Do I want a liberal-arts education, or do I have a specific career in mind for which a specific college major can prepare me? Is that vocational training all that I want from my education? Many educators and business executives prefer students with a liberal-arts education. Specific job skills can be learned at the workplace. Many professions require graduate school.

4. What is my financial situation? Can I (and my family) cope with the high tuition of a private college or university? Don't be put off by what you hear about high tuition at private colleges. For

one thing, there are many scholarships available, as well as work-study options. There are also many fine private colleges and universities with moderate tuition. Two books by Edward Fiske can point you in the right direction: *The Best Buys in College Education* and *The Selective Guide to Colleges.*

5. Do I want to stay in my home state or explore another part of the country? If you opt for the latter, be sure to figure in the cost of home visits when making out your budget. Be aware that the highest airfare and the most difficult time to book flights occur at Thanksgiving, Christmas, and Easter.

6. Will I be eligible for scholarships and financial aid?

7. Am I looking for a college that will allow me a considerable amount of choice in selecting my courses, or do I want a college where there are stiff requirements so I'll be forced to study certain subjects I might not take on my own?

8. Is there a specific college I really want to attend?

9. Is there a specific college my parents want me to attend? Is that a place I'd like to go?

10. Do my SAT (or ACT) scores really reflect my academic abilities?

11. What are my special skills and talents that would be worth noting on a college application to make me stand out from other applicants in my range?

12. Do I want to aim for a college that is very competitive academically, or one without the pressure of having to elbow my way into an A?

13. Do I want a very large, impersonal university where I can melt into the background, a small intimate college where everybody knows everybody else, or one in between?

14. Do I want a college where people come from all parts of the country or a region different from mine? Believe it or not, regional differences can be tricky, especially when it comes to food. Sprouts on a kosher corned beef sandwich on rye in Santa Cruz seemed

mighty strange to someone used to the delis of New York City. Another Yankee, who chose to go south to college, complained about grits and gravy being served every morning at breakfast.

15. Am I going to be happy in a college where fraternities and sororities are a major part of the social scene? Or, conversely, in a setting where they are not?

16. Do I want a college that offers a chance to get involved with the local community?

17. Do I need to be sure there are people who belong to the same religious faith and ethnic group as I do? Or will it be enough to know that outside the college community, I can find my own religious or ethnic group?

18. Will I want to look for organizations on campus that reflect my political ideals?

19. If I go to college far from home, will I mind not seeing my family more than once or twice a year? If the dorms close down over holiday breaks, will I have a place to stay?

20. Do I want to test the waters in a community college first before attending a high-powered four-year college?

After you've answered these questions, go back to your self-assessment test and take it again. How do the answers to these questions mesh with your profile on the assessment sheets? If you think you have a pretty good idea of what you are looking for in a college, you are ready for the next step.

INFORMATION GATHERING

There are all kinds of ways to research the college market. Even if you have been out of school for a couple of years, you may go back to your high school guidance counselor and seek her or his advice. Many schools have sophisticated software programs that can help you narrow your selection as you enter your interests, financial requirements, and other pertinent information. And you can always do your own research on the Web, although that can be a somewhat tedious process since it often presents you with more choices than you are really comfortable with.

There are numerous books and magazines that can provide you with information, including *Making a Difference College Guide,* by Miriam Weinstein, a book of selected colleges that offer courses designed to help you make the world a better place. Of course there is *Barron's Profiles of American Colleges,* which describes more than 1,500 colleges, and the many Peterson's Guides as well. Sometimes, however, these books can be overwhelming. There are other ways to explore your options, including talking to friends and relatives about their college experiences. As well, when you find a college that interests you, you can do a thorough exploration of it on the Web, and even e-mail students there to get the lowdown from a student point of view.

Ten tips for exploring colleges on the Internet

Douglas Fireside, who teachers computer skills to students, offers these suggestions.

1. Use a good search engine. A lot of the work has already been done by others. Why replicate it? Use Yahoo (http://www.yahoo.com), Google (http://www.google.com) or one of the other larger search engines to help sort things out. Follow the links they already have for finding a specific college or for other information.

2. It pays to know what you are looking for. Are you looking for information on financial aid? Do you already know an area of the country (or other countries) you are interested in researching? Are you looking for a big school or a smaller college? The Web is vast, and you can spend (or waste) a lot of time looking around. One good way to do this is to search with as many "keywords" as you can to narrow down your results. Don't just search for "colleges." Try "liberal arts colleges Maryland," for example.

3. There is a lot of FREE information about financial aid. For example, try http://www.students.gov. This links you to the federal government's higher education resource. It is designed to outline the programs that the Feds have created to help you (and/or your parents) pay for college. If you don't have Internet access, you can call the following toll-free number: (800) 4-FED-AID. Another source with a lot of info is http://www.finaid.org.

There are plenty of other places for information. A quick search turned up more than 400 sites. Again, read carefully. If you can, narrow down your search (see tip number two).

IMPORTANT: Do not pay (or give your credit card number) for information about financial aid. You can get this same information for free from other sources.

4. Use a college or university Web site for all it is worth! If you are interested in a college and would like to find out about campus life, some sites allow you to e-mail resident life directors or see which professors are teaching a program you are interested in.

5. Use the Web when you need to find specialized information. If you are looking for a traditionally African-American college, try: http://www.edonline.com/cq/hbcu/. This site connects you with historically African-American colleges and universities. It also has information on finding financial aid.

Looking for women's colleges? Try using Yahoo. A quick search turned up an impressive list of sites.

6. Not sure where to start? Try this site: http://www.globalcomputing.com/universy.html. This site allows you to check a lot of the college Web sites by clicking on a region of the country. It's a great way to cut through the clutter. Simply click on a state and a list comes up!

7. Some schools have multiple sites. Some have e-mail links that allow you to contact students and professors. Some list entrance requirements, financial aid information, etc. CAUTION:

Don't judge a school solely by its Web site. Call and talk to alums or current students. Best yet, visit the school.

8. If a school doesn't have the information you need on its site, don't give up. Get a nice new notebook to use for your Web searches. Take notes. Write down phone numbers and addresses of schools that look interesting to you. Schools are happy to send you information by snail mail.

9. Remember that Web sites change faster than search engines can keep up. Most school sites stay around, but their content changes. It pays to check back if you visited a site more than a month ago. Links to "campus life" areas might change frequently—some of these link up to businesses near the school.

10. Read the FAQ for a school or other education site.

Gerard Turbide, senior assistant director of admissions at Ithaca College in New York, says that the advantage of seeking out information about a college online is the interactive flavor. "A big plus is that you can have contact with faculty and students." He also notes the advantage a prospective student has of being able to get information in a very flexible manner, i.e., he or she can get the information about a college at any time—10 P.M. or midnight, if that works. Turbide stresses that all e-mail sent to the admissions office is read and answered personally by admissions counselors. But he also points out that nothing replaces a campus visit, although the virtual college tour is a nice complement to the real thing.

SHOULD I SEEK OUT A COLLEGE CONSULTANT?

You may also want to find a professional educational consultant who is trained to help you find the right college (consultants will charge a fee). Guided by your interests, SAT or ACT scores, and personality, a consultant can take a lot of the guesswork out of the process. A good consultant focuses on your individual needs, has lots of experience in helping students find a suitable college, has visited at least 100 colleges and universities around the country, and is up to date on at least as many others. Of course, anybody can have business cards printed and call him or herself a "college consultant"—so you have to shop carefully. You want a consultant who is not only skilled in helping you find the right school but who also continually updates his or her knowledge of the college scene.

> **"Anybody can have business cards printed and call him or herself a 'college consultant.'"**

One organization that will provide you with a list of professional educational consultants is the Independent Educational Consultants Association (IECA). You can contact the Association at 3251 Old Lee Highway, Suite 510, Fairfax, VA, 22030, (703) 591-4850, (703) 591-4860, iecaassoc@aol.com, http://www. educationalconsulting.org.

Although most people do just fine on their own or with help from their high school guidance counselors or friends, there are situations when a college consultant can be of enormous help.

Mark Sklarow, executive director of IECA, says, "Nobody really knows everything about the thousands of college and post-high school programs that are out there. A good educational consultant is an expert matchmaker. He or she can help you figure out your particular needs." Members of IECA are constantly updating their information by visiting campuses, taking workshops, and sharing information with other members. Many consultants specialize in certain areas, such as placing students with disabilities or special needs.

If you and your parents seem to be at odds over the colleges you are choosing, or if you are looking for an interesting program before you go off to college, a consultant can help you and your family sort things out. If you really aren't at all sure where you would fit in, a college consultant can help.

SPECIAL SITUATIONS

Perhaps the best reason to choose a consultant is if you are a person with special needs, such as being gifted and talented; have had a nontraditional education, such as attending alternative schools; have been homeschooled; or are challenged by a specific learning or physical disability. Because people with disabilities are guaranteed their civil rights by federal law, every college that receives federal funds must provide some special support services and accommodations for students with disabilities. Thus, while many colleges will tell you they have special programs, it can take an expert to evaluate them. A savvy consultant can save you endless months of frustration.

The following is a clearinghouse on postsecondary education for individuals with disabilities and is funded by the U.S. Department of Education.

Heath Resource Center
The George Washington University
2121 K Street, NW, Suite 220
Washington, DC 20037
(202) 973-0904 or
(800) 544-3284 (Voice TT available)
http://www.acenet.edu

IF YOU HAVE BEEN HOMESCHOOLED

If you are one of the many students who have been uniquely educated either at home or in a nontraditional school setting, you will find that much of the college application form simply doesn't apply to you. And you will have to find a way to prove to the admissions committee that you are ready and qualified to pursue a college degree. This is where you will want to get as much information as possible from the admissions officers before you file your application. Without traditional grades to show to a prospective college, or without your teacher recommendations to add, you will have to rely on two things: your personal essay and your SAT or ACT scores. You might also want to find out whether the colleges you are applying to will be willing to look at a portfolio of your work. "Homeschooled students present all sorts of interesting problems," says Sklarow, and in his discussions with admissions officers, he finds that they "are trying to figure out how to fit them in." He finds that most colleges are accepting small numbers of homeschooled students—but it is up to the student to show that he or she has acquired the skills needed to succeed. Check out this Web site: www.homeschool.com/advisors/mckee.

Oona Grady DeFlaun was homeschooled along with her siblings and cousins. Her parents, aunts, and uncles joined a group known as the Finger Lakes Home Schoolers Network. "We have a bimonthly newsletter," said Oona. It reports the various activities being organized by the parents and kids. If some of the homeschooled kids want to study a particular subject, they put an announcement in the newsletter.

"The most regular activity I did was music." Starting at age four, Oona studied violin. "Eventually, it became what I did. I remember saying I didn't want to do it anymore when I was little, so my mother would say, 'Ok, call up your teacher and tell her that.' Of course I didn't. In the past couple of years it was really something I loved. When I was ten or eleven, our family friend who played the Irish fiddle began to teach me some Irish songs. Now I take lessons from him every week."

Along with her cousin Marie, who plays the pennywhistle and flute, the girls took part in a *flaeugh*—it's a competition for a

Cheouil which is a festival of Irish music. In 2001 both Oona and Marie went to New York City for a competition. Those who placed first or second were sent to Ireland to compete there. Oona came in second in solo fiddle and won a scholarship to Ireland. Marie didn't make the cut that year, but she was able to get a cheap plane ticket and went along with Oona. "We stayed with some family friends, and it was a strange and wonderful experience." The second year they competed in New York City, "we placed first in every category." This time Oona placed first in solo violin, while Marie placed first in flute and pennywhistle. "So again we went to Ireland. We never placed over there. This year we won the New York City competition again," she said. But before they go off to Ireland, Oona and Marie are going to the Rocky Mountain Fiddle contest. "It's all fiddle and flute music. Some famous teachers will be there, and then we will go to Ireland, take more classes, and compete again." Oona said that competing wasn't her favorite part. "It's making connections with other people. There are a few hundred thousand people who come to this event—the entire town [is involved]."

Oona decided to apply to college when she turned eighteen. "This whole college thing. Well, it's not like I have any great ambitions. It's more like I've never gone to school, and it would be sort of interesting to do that kind of thing. I should try it out."

Her approach to choosing a college was to talk to friends and relatives about their college experiences. She narrowed it down to three: Oberlin, Smith, and her mother's alma mater, Beloit. "I used the common application, and I had to fill out a lot of forms. I wrote my essay on three things that were unique about me." Oona comes from a very unusual family. All, including her grandparents on her father's side, have been engaged in nonviolent war protest, going back to the Vietnam war. Virtually every one of the adults in her family has been jailed at one time or another for his or her actions. So Oona wrote about her family's involvement in nonviolent protest, her interest in Irish music and the fact that she's been home schooled. Since she didn't have transcripts, she typed up a list of the projects she had completed, internships she did, and books she read. Although she didn't do especially well on her SATs, she was admitted to Smith and Beloit. She chose Beloit because it offered her an excellent scholarship. However, Oona is delaying college for a year to work on her music. And to carry on the family tradition of nonviolent antiwar protest.

CHECK OUT COLLEGE CATALOGS

Once you have an idea of several colleges you'd like to apply to, you can spend some time reading through a variety of college catalogs or viewbooks. Both Internet and hard copy have their advantages and disadvantages. You can request a paper catalog directly from specific colleges or check them out of your public library or school guidance office. Make sure you get current catalogs. (After your SAT or ACT scores are in, your mailbox will be filled with them.) While catalogs tell you what courses are offered, viewbooks show you something else.

You can see what the campus looks like, the kinds of students it attracts (all have smiling students), the academic priorities, the fees, the living arrangements, the outside activities, and much more.

Rodney Christopher remarks that the viewbook from Simon's Rock was very "inviting." He had never heard of the college before, but after reading through it, he was eager for the next step: a campus visit.

When Doug Leonard decided to head south to study in North Carolina, he sent for several viewbooks and narrowed his choices to two possibilities. "I did this on the basis of the city where I wanted to be, the size of the school I thought would be best for me, and the kinds of courses they had to offer. Of course, the fact that the University of North Carolina in Greensboro had a ratio of three women for every man was definitely part of the equation," he notes with a happy grin. "And that last bit of information was in the viewbook."

How to read college viewbooks and catalogs

College catalogs and viewbooks are meant to entice you. Viewbooks are filled with photos of beautiful buildings, laughing students, and winning athletic teams. Viewbooks are advertisements for the college. College catalogs, on the other hand, offer a great deal of solid information. For example, in a catalog you can find out:

➤ How many professors have Ph.D.'s; how many are full-time members of the faculty and how many are part-time "adjunct professors"
➤ From which colleges the professors graduated
➤ The student-faculty ratio
➤ Whether the department you are interested in has enough professors who reflect different viewpoints (this can be learned from the kinds of courses offered, as well as the universities that trained the professors)
➤ Whether there is a core curriculum
➤ Whether there is an overall philosophy in the college
➤ Whether there is a multicultural approach to learning and to the student body
➤ Whether there is a study-abroad program
➤ Whether there is an honor society

Viewbooks will give you a different look at the college. You can find out:
➤ Whether there are extracurricular activities that appeal to you
➤ Whether there are requirements you feel are not what you need or want

➤ Whether transfer credit from summer college courses or study abroad is obtainable

➤ Whether there is a senior honors project

➤ Whether off-campus internships are available

➤ Whether there are adequate library resources or access to other nearby college libraries

➤ Whether there is a physical education requirement

➤ Whether writing skills are emphasized

➤ Whether the size and location of the school is right for you

➤ Whether the religious, racial, or ethnic group you belong to is represented on campus

➤ Whether the price tag is within your target range

➤ Whether adequate financial aid is available

Even if you are savvy enough to dig out all of the good information in the viewbook or course catalog they alone will not tell you everything. Check out some college guidebooks. They will tell you how competitive the colleges are. *Profiles of American Colleges* ranks colleges by most competitive, highly competitive, very competitive and competitive, less competitive, noncompetitive, and special. (This last category is made up of professional schools of music and art.) Finally, go to the Web site of the college you are interested in for more information.

Are campus visits important?

If there are two or three colleges that interest you in one area, you can arrange several campus visits during the same week. Phone, write, or e-mail the admissions office to request a campus tour. Some colleges require appointments, but at others you can just stop in the admissions office and a tour will be arranged on the spot. If you come with your parents, they, of course, will have a different agenda than you. Make sure you have the opportunity to see and talk about the things you are interested in. David DeVries, associate dean for undergraduate education at Cornell University, cautions students to think about what interests them before they visit. Students may want to focus on living arrangements—the relationships between dorm activities and academics, for example. He suggests that it will be important for you to know where you can go for advising on campus, where to go if you become ill, or where to go if you need emotional support during a difficult time. Remember that once you arrive on a college campus, you will be on your own, without the usual support system you had at home. You should talk to as many students and staff as possible. "But," DeVries says, "be prepared to hear the same thing differently from students and adults. Not everything people say is true!" For example, he said, a student guide may have just been dragged out of bed to do a tour and may not be in the best of spirits on a given day.

Don't be afraid to talk with professors. You are the reason they have a job! And if you are interested in their subject, they love to talk about their work. It helps, of course, if you've read something they have written and mention it. You will have made their day.

> "Don't be afraid to talk to professors. You are the reason they have a job!"

Most colleges will have a variety of sessions that you can attend. Go to as many as you can fit in. But be sure that you go to sessions where your interests will be discussed.

Visiting several colleges during a short period gives a person the chance to see differences, both good and bad. If you wish, you can arrange to stay overnight in a dorm—but you will need to reserve that in advance of your visit.

And when you show up for a campus visit, dress casually, but keep your shirttails tucked in and wear comfortable walking shoes.

Checking out several colleges during a single week proved extremely helpful to Doug. Among his North Carolina possibilities was one in Raleigh. He had already been accepted there before he visited the campus. "I was really disappointed once I saw the place," Doug says. "Even though I'd written ahead and phoned to make sure the admissions people knew I was coming, when I got there they seemed totally disinterested in me. They did nothing to make me want to go there. On the other hand, from the moment I set foot on the UNC campus at Greensboro, I felt at home. Everybody, from the admissions people to the students and the professors I talked to, seemed to want me to come here. One of the professors in my field of communications had read my application. She even remembered that I'd had some experience as a DJ back home. 'I can't wait until you come here,' she said. She really made me feel as if my time away from school was well spent.

"It was such a welcoming atmosphere. I knew this was the place for me. Even though it was a fairly small campus, Greensboro is a real city, and there seemed to be a lot of stuff going on there."

Doug's perception of the university and the city proved correct for his objectives. Over the years he made strong friendships, took classes that were both enjoyable and challenging—and found time to start a weekly newspaper with a group of like-minded students. One summer he remained in Greensboro to work at a local radio station and study. He got a kick out of conducting campus tours for prospective students. "As a Yankee, I wanted to be able to return the kind of hospitality I'd received." After Doug graduated from UNC-G, he spent a

> "It was such a welcoming atmosphere. I knew this was the place for me."

year working at a television station in Raleigh and at the radio station where he'd interned.

HOW MANY COLLEGES SHOULD I APPLY TO?

Until a few years ago, most college-bound students felt safe applying to three or four colleges. One of these was often called the "safety" school—such as the nearest state university. Today, however, students often apply to 10 or 15 colleges! At $40 or more for filing each application, that can be quite a hefty sum of money. (For students with very limited financial resources, this application fee is often waived.) College admissions officers have no way of knowing which students are applying to a dozen or more colleges. In addition, applications are coming from students who, until recently, might not have considered a college education. These "newcomers" are highly qualified because more and more people recognize that if they are going to be eligible for higher paying jobs, they will need that college diploma. Moreover, colleges and universities are actively recruiting minorities, students with disabilities, and foreign students. Bringing in bright, qualified students who once believed college was not within their reach is a very exciting prospect. It assures a greater diversity on college campuses and benefits everybody.

THE IMPORTANCE OF PLANNING

Many high school seniors are shocked to discover they have not been accepted into any college. Even students with terrific SAT scores and grades from excellent high schools can be left out in the cold, although by midsummer many of these students apply to a second round of colleges and find one to take them, or decide to stop out for a year.

But why would you want to take an online course rather than a course with a professor, face-to-face in a real classroom, with real students to interact with?

Perhaps you will be doing a semester or a year abroad and your favorite college professor is offering a course you especially want to take. You can take that course, as long as you have Internet access.

Or perhaps, like Kristen Thomas, you cannot be on campus all the time. Taking courses online while in another part of the country means you will be able to graduate in a reasonable amount of time without taking a leave of absence.

Shortly after Kristen graduated from high school, she married her high school sweetheart. Her husband joined the Marines, and Kristen followed him to Camp Lejune in North Carolina, where she became a full-time homemaker and the mother of a son. The first time her husband was deployed overseas for six months, Kristen and her son moved back to Candor, New York, to stay with her mom, who offered to take care of her son. Kristen had decided it was time to think about a career in nursing, but with a young child, going to school was going to be especially difficult when she rejoined her husband. "Then I heard about the SUNY Learning Network [SLN] through Tompkins-Cortland Community College [TC-3]." Kristen discovered that she could take some of her courses at the community college during the months she was staying with her mother, and some of her courses online when she was back in North Carolina—or wherever her husband was stationed.

"My nursing courses I will take face-to-face, but my SLN courses are basics. This is the first semester I'm doing the SLN courses, and," she notes, "it has had its ups and downs. It's good if the professor is very clear on what he or she wants. We've been having problems with one professor, though. This professor just tells you what to read and doesn't answer his e-mail, and also, he doesn't post discussion questions."

There can be other problems, too. "Sometimes you have computer problems, or the server is down, or something like that. But, on balance, this is a great way for me to get my education. I'm always on the computer. I'm always checking my e-mail to see what my classmates have said in their discussions, and then I will reply to them." Kristen also likes the fact that while there are deadlines she has to meet, there is no set time for her to get online.

"You know, when I was a student in high school, I goofed off a lot. But being away from home, with a son, I realized that I need my education, and it's hard to get this education and try to find good day care down here. The SLN courses are a godsend.

"It's just as if it were face-to-face. It's almost like chatting, only you can't see the person."

> "One thing we've already found out is that the success rate of people completing online courses is 90 percent!"

Kristen is one of many students getting part, if not all, of her education on the Web. At New York University, for example, there are more than 20,000 students enrolled in online courses. According to Dr. Kathleen McKee, vice president of academic affairs at Neumann College, there still needs to be much research done on how well the Internet delivers education. "One thing we've already found out is that the success rate of people completing online courses is 90 percent!"

NEW TECHNOLOGY REACHES INTO THE CLASSROOM

Distance learning doesn't happen only through the Internet. Some colleges, especially small colleges, have begun to offer classes to partner colleges through a video conferencing technology called PictureTel. Dr. Rosalie Merenda, president of Neumann College in Pennsylvania, is very enthusiastic about using the new technology because it "is an opportunity to offer classes where there may not be enough students in one college. Technology offers a way to bring about diversity and quality. We need the technology as an option."

> **Distance learning doesn't happen only through the Internet.**

Neumann has entered into a partnership with Beaver College to offer certain elective courses via PictureTel. Bill Lynch is a professor of English at Neumann College. He has been teaching courses in English literature, theater, and film for nearly 30 years. He loves the challenge of teaching using television. "It's rather like juggling with four or five different balls and trying to keep them up in the air. You have to deal with course content; you have to try to read the faces of the students in front of you and get feedback from them as to what they understand, and you've got to do the same thing for the people on the other end. You've got students in two locations, and you function as a kind of director . . . as you handle the visuals in terms of pushing the right buttons to get the right camera."

Michael Criscuolo is majoring in English at Neumann College and takes the interactive course in theater with Dr. Lynch. "It's different and new, and very worthwhile," he says. "I especially like working with Joyce and John from Beaver College. They are older students—middle-aged folks—and it is nice to interact with them. Also, we get to share our own experiences as we read the assignments. Older students have a different perspective from the younger students at Neumann. We're all around the same age— 19 or 20. Joyce is also an English major, and she has read so much more than I have. I feel as if I'm working much harder in this class."

"It's different and new, and very worthwhile."

The downside to the videoconferencing, however, is obvious to Michael. "During our break, the students who are in the same room with Professor Lynch can talk to him, but the students at Beaver College can't. And another problem is that when one of us presents an oral report, there is an echo on our end, and that's disconcerting. Finally, those at Beaver have only one monitor. We have two. So if the professor is using the overhead, they can only see what's on that screen. They can hear, but they can't see anything else."

Dr. Merenda recognizes that interactive and online courses offer many challenges. "Not all of the paradigms will work. Technology offers wonderful options, and we are taking baby steps here. There is a lot to learn."

The exciting thing for you as a college student in the 21st century is that you have options that no other generation of young people have had in the way you can pursue your education. The most important thing you can do for yourself is to be aware of your strengths and weaknesses—and be honest about them. Don't put yourself down, but don't get a swelled head either. College can be a grand adventure. Not only will you meet wonderful people, encounter ideas and subjects that you never dreamed about, and learn how to think and reason, but you will also be giving yourself a gift that is yours forever. No one can ever take away your education. It is the single experience that pays dividends over your entire lifetime and can provide you with untold years of pleasure.

Chapter X

What If College Isn't for Me? The UnCollege Option

ARE YOU ONE OF THOSE PEOPLE WHO CAN HONESTLY SAY THAT HIGH SCHOOL JUST DIDN'T WORK FOR YOU? That book learning really turned you off? Would you describe yourself as a "hands-on learner"? One of those people who can take things apart and put them back together almost without looking at the directions? Or did you do OK in high school, but your heart really wasn't in it, and the prospect of four or even two years of college makes you ill?

Is it true that if you don't go to college (as your parents and teachers have told you) you'll be stuck flipping hamburgers at Burger King or stocking shelves at Wal-Mart? The answer truly is not an "either/or."

You actually have many other choices.

Perhaps you are a person who would do well to look into a skilled trade. Today many jobs are being outsourced to India, China, Mexico, and other foreign countries. But if you develop a skill that can't be outsourced, you can look forward to a satisfying career that will pay an excellent wage.

Listen up: No matter where in the world a car is manufactured, if you need repair work done, it has to be done where you live. If the local college is building new dorms, someone has to wire the electricity, put in the heating and water lines, and construct the actual building. If the roof on your house leaks, someone nearby has to fix it. If you want the smartest hairstyle, or perhaps a complete makeover at a spa, chances are you can get that right where you live. And if such a place doesn't yet exist in your town, you might be just the person to make it happen. None of those jobs can be outsourced. It's got to be done on the spot.

A PORTABLE PROFESSION

Brian Millspaugh knew that he "wasn't much for learning out of books." He did all right—basically he was a B student, but in his junior year at Trumansburg (New York) High School, he had the option of going to BOCES (Board of Cooperative Education Service) for technical training. "I took residential electric up there, and in my senior year I learned commercial electrical work." In the morning Brian took regular classes at his high school. In the afternoons he was bused to the BOCES classes.

Brian was brought up around carpenters all of his life. "My dad owns a lumber company in Trumansburg, and I guess that this [electrical work] was the one trade that my family didn't know too well. And it was a free education, so I took it, and I loved it." Brian graduated from his own high school with a Regents diploma and decided that he had two options. His first choice was to get into the electricians' union, and he put in his application right after graduation. He figured that if he didn't make the cut, he'd join the Air Force.

At the end of the summer, Brian took the written test for admission into the union's apprentice program. After a pretty intense personal interview, he learned he was one of just four people hired as an apprentice. This is a five-year, on-the-job training program. Apprentices work a 40-hour week, and they must take formal classes one evening every week. All through the training period Brian gets paid "decent wages and all medical benefits." He began his apprenticeship by making $11.13 an hour. Each year he gets regular raises. By the time he finishes his apprenticeship to become a journeyman, his salary will go up to over $25 per hour. He must attend classes every Monday night from 4:20 P.M. until 9 P.M. or 9:30 P.M. Some of the classes are held at the electrical shop at Cornell University. If he ever decides to enroll in a college, he will be able to transfer some of his courses toward a bachelor's degree in electrical engineering.

Brian points out that there hasn't been a layoff in over ten years, and most of the time the local union has to recruit electricians from other locals. Brian loves the special camaraderie that develops among the workers. "Everybody you work with goes through the same stuff, and everybody goes out of their way to teach you stuff. If you're willing to learn, you've got everything there."

Probably the hardest part of the job was knowing that "if I don't get to work on time, I don't have a job. You know, when you're in high school, you get up at 7:30 in the morning and you go to school till 2:30. Now I'm up at 5:30 every morning and go to work. School is like an option. But here you have to work hard in order to succeed."

When Brian's old friends come home from college, they expect him to hang out with them until all hours of the night. "And I can't do that," he said. "I won't be able to get up for work." On the other hand, "they are a bit jealous. I'm earning money and they're not. I have a nice car, and some nice toys, and they have college debts."

As he looks toward the future, Brian notes that while he loves living in upstate New York, he will have a "portable profession." After he completes his apprenticeship, he can go anywhere. "Union work is all around the United States—from New York to California."

In order to find the International Brotherhood of Electrical Workers in your community, check the Yellow Pages under Labor Unions. Or go to http://www.njact.org/apprentice.html.

To be considered for the apprenticeship program, you must have a high school diploma or a GED and at least one year of algebra. Says Brian, "You don't have to 'know' someone." You do have to take a written test in reading and math and undergo an interview.

Many unions are actively seeking women and people of color because when government contracts are given out, unions that can show they can attract these populations are the ones who get the jobs.

IT'S NOT THE GREASE MONKEY THING

Robin Walker is now 23 years old and lives in Spring, Texas, not far from Houston. After he graduated from high school he enrolled in the local community college. "That didn't really satisfy me. For one thing, it took too long to get a degree (I'm not a patient person), and then when you get the degree, you're really not going to earn much money." So Robin decided he was better off working on cars. "I've always had a passion for cars," he says. When a friend suggested he check out the Universal Technical Institute (which, in addition to its Houston location, has campuses in California, Arizona, and Illinois), Robin found that UTI suited his goals perfectly. He signed up for the automotive program, finishing it in six and a half months instead of the usual nine. "That's because I took courses both during the day and in the evenings. Then I applied to take the 'elite' program." That was a four-month course in which he learned to work on Mercedes-Benz cars. This course took place at a separate campus and was taught by the staff from the Mercedes-Benz company. "In order to get into the program," Robin says, "your attendance has to be excellent and your grades have to be good." At the end of the elite course, Robin was hired by the Houston Mercedes-Benz dealership. He's set his sights on earning upwards of $70,000 a year. "The reason why," he says, "is that the way your hours are counted are not 'physical hours.' The hours are determined by the job itself. So if you are fast, you can make a lot of money. But if you are lollygagging around, you won't make as much."

A LAST CHANCE

A couple of years ago Brad Herndon's dad worried that his son would never graduate from high school, let alone wind up with a good paying job in a field he loves. From the time he was in middle school, Brad was doing drugs and abusing alcohol. At one point, worried that Brad would do irreparable harm to himself, Ken Herndon had his son arrested and brought into court. Brad got sent to rehab and managed to graduate from high school. "But then," says Brad, "I did something else. When I was 18 I got caught breaking and entering, and wound up on probation."

His dad, however, never gave up on him. "I knew that Brad was a hands-on learner," he says, so he and Brad started researching places where Brad could learn a solid skill. Auto mechanics seemed like the right choice. "I was interested in cars when I was younger," Brad says. "I had a Honda Civic and I fixed it up myself."

Brad and his dad visited several dealerships in the New Jersey area, where they lived, and people kept telling them that UTI in Houston was the best in the country. UTI sent a representative to interview Brad "to see if I was good enough to go to school [there]." The representative questioned Brad about his drug and alcohol use, and whether or not he'd been in jail. Brad's father says, "Based on the kinds of questions asked and answered, it was determined that Brad would be a good candidate for their school." UTI has a strict drug policy, and students know that there will be random drug tests. Brad was tested every three weeks.

When Ken Herndon dropped his son off in Houston to be on his own, he wondered whether Brad would make it at UTI.

Brad had his doubts, too. "When I first got to Houston, it was so hot [it was August]! And I was still on probation—and Houston wasn't anything like a small town in Jersey." At one point he had to return to New Jersey for his court appearance, and when he got back to Houston, the New Jersey authorities had checked up on him. "I didn't get into any trouble there," he says, "and I've been clean for almost two years now."

UTI turned out to be just the right place for Brad. "It was real easy to make friends down there. At first I was assigned housing with three other kids, and there were around ten kids in my class from my neighborhood." The classes were absolutely first-rate. "If you already have a basic knowledge of cars, they give you plenty of extra help, and the teachers are amazing. I'd come to school at 6 A.M. and the classes wouldn't start until 7, and the teachers would be there to help me. They were waiting for you."

In addition to enjoying the classes (which are offered three different times daily, so that people who are working can fit classes into any schedule), Brad found it easy to find work. "They have bulletin boards with notices of who is hiring. When I was there I had six jobs all within a year."

Brad trained on collision, repair, and refinishing. When he completed the 11-and-a-half-month course (courses vary in length according to the specific area of study), he took the certification tests and passed with flying colors. "I took some extra classes, and I was always practicing and studying while some other kids weren't, and I came out with more points then they did. This," Brad knew, "was my last chance."

When he returned to New Jersey, he brought his course catalog, his grades, and his certification. "It took me only two days to find a job." He had five offers! "I'm working for a collision company right now. It's a really good company, with good benefits." He

Technician Training

Universal Technical Institute trains people to become technicians on a variety of vehicles, including motorcycles, watercraft, automobiles, and trucks. To contact the Texas campus: Universal Technical Institute; Texas Campus; 721 Lockhaven Dr., Houston, TX, 77073, (800) 325-0354. Tuition costs vary with the length of the course—anywhere from $21,000 to $31,150, plus living expenses. The Institute is fully accredited and financial aid is available.

To learn more about UTI, visit http://www.uticorp.com.

expects to earn around $35,000 the first year. Like Robin, he is on an hourly flat rate, so that as he works faster, he will make more money. "I still have a lot of learning to do. The guys [where he works] help you out a lot. They teach you things the school doesn't. The school teaches you a really good method of doing things, but there are a 100 different ways to do the same job."

Brad's last chance paid off. "I have my own apartment. I'm living with my fiancée. I now have my own car, and pay my own car insurance. I don't need any help from my parents now." Indeed, he doesn't. Brad is making excellent money; he has medical and dental insurance, plus a 401(k), stock options, and life insurance . . . and a bright future.

WHO DOES WELL AT UTI?

Chery Geggleman, director of employment at UTI in Houston, says, "The kid who does well at UTI is the one who can take direction. What the employers tell us is that they need to look like this: They have to dress appropriately and know how to serve the public. They have to have a positive attitude. We make our dress code and our rules on campus based on what the business world wants. The most successful graduates here come in and keep their eye on the goal, and they walk out of the door and have multiple job offers."

Robin Walker says, "It's really important to have an open mind. And if you're 18 or 19 and you've never been away before, you might not know what to do without Mom and Dad around—and you can get into a lot of trouble. But if you are really ambitious and have the same attitude that I had, that's the way to do it. You need to want to learn. The information is there. Well, perhaps a teacher doesn't know everything, but you have to expect that. If you want to learn, you read the book and have discussions."

A BUSINESS OF HER OWN

No one would have thought that Barrie French would become a successful businesswoman when she quit high school, least of all Barrie herself. "I never liked school," she said. "I did like the social scene, and that was about it. Nothing interested me except art and music and photography. History and math didn't do anything for me." By the time she'd turned 16, she'd cut so many classes, she decided to simply drop out and get a place of her own and a job. Two years later, Barrie started commuting to cosmetology school in Syracuse, New York, from her apartment in Ithaca. Because she didn't own a car, she rode with two other women. But the women graduated four months before Barrie was to finish, and once again, Barrie dropped out of school. For a while she waitressed and bartended. Eventually, however, she decided to finish what she'd started and was able to complete her cosmetology course at the local BOCES in Ithaca.

Barrie worked in a beauty salon for about a year and a half, and then she decided to open her own salon.

"It was exciting. A lot of people asked me if I was very nervous. But honestly, I wasn't. I just came up with a business plan by taking figures on what I was making part time as a hair stylist in a salon and then I doubled that because I'd be working in my own shop full-time. Fortunately, I had access to my former boss's bills for gas and electric and products and rent and all that. I based my plan on what she brought in and what she paid out. When I went to the bank, they said it was a great business plan and everything looked wonderful." However, the bank still didn't want to give Barrie a loan without a cosigner, so her father cosigned on it. Her original loan was for $13,000.

That surely didn't sound like a lot of money with which to start a business from scratch. However, Barrie was both resourceful and realistic. She settled for an excellent location, but in the basement rather than a street-level shop. "I used my sources for buying secondhand. I found a couch for the waiting area that was in great shape but the cover was awful, so my mom and I recovered it. I bought all of my contents and everything I needed to run the operation, plus four months' worth of rent, and had money left over. I had to have plumbers and carpenters and rooms installed, and I'm good with budgeting my money. That's why I never really thought for a moment, 'What if it doesn't make it?'"

With such careful planning, Barrie had about $4,000 left over. "It cost me just $9,000 for everything else to start up. People were surprised that I got away with this with not finishing high school and not having had business experience. But it's because I wanted to do it, so I went at it full force."

The first year Barrie managed to make money and pay all of her bills. She continually added to her cushion of money. She improved her business as she went along. She found that the best advertising was word of mouth and satisfied customers. She settled on one particular brand of hair product, and then added skin care and makeup to her retail sale items. When her hair business suddenly took off, her retail sales jumped over 150 percent because she carried an excellent product that was well known.

Barrie French has now been in business for ten years. Today she employs seven people. She has expanded her salon space twice and has recently taken over what was once an ice-cream shop upstairs, where she opened a women's clothing shop. She also carries a line of jewelry, which she herself creates. "I've made jewelry for many years just as a hobby and for friends. Then I started selling it here." When she first began her venture, she worked six days a week. Now she works just three.

"After I paid off the $13,000 loan—[the payment] was $189 a month—I figured I'd never miss that money, so I topped it off at $200 and opened an IRA so I'd have some sort of savings."

So what are some of the traits that have made Barrie French successful?

➤ "I'm a gutsy person," she says.
➤ She's outgoing and friendly.
➤ She genuinely likes people.
➤ She offers her customers special "presents" for their birthdays and anniversaries, such as discounts on haircuts or other services.
➤ She is very careful with money and plans ahead.
➤ She sets realistic goals for herself and her staff.
➤ Once she recognized the need for training, she completed her course.
➤ She spent time working for someone else so she could learn the business from the inside out.

Not having a high school diploma "bothered me for a while, but not now." As she considers her next step, she is thinking about "getting into interior design and organizing special events. I'd like to become a party planner. And of course, I'm still plugging away at the jewelry. Themes and decorating," she says, really interest her. "And I now have my own house which will be turned into a bed and breakfast soon. I like the challenge of it."

"I KNEW WHERE I WAS GOING"

Christoph Stucker started working in the restaurant industry when he was 14. "I started out as a dishwasher," he said. It was a small restaurant inside the owner's house. "He was Italian, and a great guy." That early experience whetted Christoph's appetite. At first he just "watched cooks do their thing. And it caught my eye. I'm a very hands-on person. I learn by doing."

The area where Christoph grew up, in the Berkshire Mountains of Massachusetts, is a vacation spot in both summer and winter, and there are many fine restaurants and inns. By the time he had graduated from Monument Mountain High School in Great Barrington, he'd done internships in most of the best restaurants in the area. At one inn, he "learned to prepare breakfast for 120 people, to multitask, and to be efficient. By the time I was accepted at the Culinary Institute in Burlington, Vermont, I knew where I was going, not like a lot of kids who didn't know what they were going to do."

The two-year program in Burlington consisted of six months of school and then a six-month internship each year. Christoph's first internship took him to a "primo restaurant in Lakeview, Connecticut, where a lot of celebrities ate." His second year's internship gave him the opportunity to go to a little village north of Frankfurt, Germany. It was his mother's hometown. "I was raised to speak German until the age of 12," he said. He lived with his aunt and uncle and worked in a large sourdough bread bakery. Since he was just an intern, he wasn't permitted to be in the bakery until 7:30 A.M., long after the dough had been made. But, Christoph said, "We would roll it out and knead it. Most of it was hand-rolled. We had wooden form baskets that we put the dough in. Then we covered it

Christoph Stucker being congratulated by his German master baker and pastry chef, Herrn Stappel, during his internship in Woerth/Main, Germany (Christoph Stucker)

with plastic sheets and let it rise." After it was baked, he would help take it around to the various stores in the area.

Christoph had a life-changing experience at the culinary school. One of the cooking classes he took was in cooking for a vegan diet. This special manner of cooking excludes all dairy products as well as all meat, fish, and poultry. "That was the thing that changed my life. I'm a vegan now." It certainly was difficult maintaining this diet while he was in Germany. The big meal there was at noontime, so Christoph would go to his grandparents' house for lunch. "They thought it was sort of strange to eat as a vegan. There were some stores where I could buy my tofu, but it's not the norm."

After graduation, Christoph opened a little restaurant in North Adams, Massachusetts. But after two months, he and the owner decided to split. He then worked at a ritzy health spa, and later became a leader in an Outward Bound program. He was having trouble deciding whether to continue on with his culinary career or to go into outdoor leadership programs. Just as he was trying to make up his mind, his parents opened a special community in North Carolina called Cooper Riis, A Healing Farm Community, for people with emotional problems. Christoph's father offered him a job as the sous chef. "I accepted the offer," he said.

"I was born and raised for nine years on Gould Farm in Great Barrington." This is one of the oldest healing communities, and Christoph's parents had both worked there. Once his parents opened Cooper Riis, one of his sisters decided to work there, too. For now, this feels just right to Christoph.

There are many different kinds of culinary schools throughout the country. They vary in cost, length of time to complete the course, and the kind of cooking you will learn. Beginning salaries are not high—most start at approximately $22,000 to $23,000 per year. Some schools offer paid internships as part of the package. You can find out more by logging on to http://www.shawguides.com.

So, is there a common thread that runs through these profiles? For one thing, these people seemed to have either a passion for or a very strong interest in something other than college. Brad and Robin both loved cars. Brian didn't know until he tried it, but found he loved the kind of work electricians do. Christoph was eager to learn all he could about food preparation, and Barrie found her niche as a beautician and a successful business owner.

Sometimes it wasn't easy getting to the right place. Yet it's entirely possible to come out on top even if you've made some serious mistakes early in your life. And one of the great things about being young today is that fields that were once the province of one gender or another are now open to both men and women. The important thing is to find something you truly love and go for it.

For more information on salaries for specific jobs in different cities and towns all over the country, log on to http://swz-hotjobs.salary.com.

Looking through lists and lists of colleges can be a daunting undertaking. With so many choices, it's not surprising that many people get frustrated and confused, and one can spend hours cruising the Internet, only to turn up poorly organized Web sites that don't tell you what you need to know. I hope that you will explore some of the colleges mentioned throughout this book. If you are looking to be admitted to college before you graduate high school, check out Chapter VIII for a start. But do remember that many other colleges and universities will admit younger students, too.

Take time to consider your college options and talk to people who have enrolled in a college you are interested in. I'm including a short and very personal list of colleges that offer something special. Use my list as a jumping off place with which to begin your search. And don't be put off by the cost. Remember, there are many opportunities for financial aid and scholarships, and your education will repay you many times over during your lifetime.

Alfred University, 1 Saxon Drive Alfred, NY, 14802, (607) 871-2111, http://www.alfred.edu. Alfred has a worldwide reputation in the fields of applied arts and engineering. With only 2,400 students, each one receives lots of personal attention.
Appalachian State University, Boone, NC, 28608, (828) 262-2000, http://www.appstate.edu. A small liberal-arts college that is part of the state university system. Within the university is Watauga College, which attracts about 100 students who live and study apart from the rest of the university. Those enrolled at Watauga design their own major fields of study.

Beloit College, 700 College Street, Beloit, WI, 53511, (608) 363-2000, http://www.beloit.edu. Beloit has unique study programs where students can get practical experience in such areas as urban studies in Chicago, or do scientific research at the Associated Colleges of the Midwest (ACM), as well as many other choices. Excellent study-abroad program as well.

Bennington College, One College Drive, Bennington, VT, 05201, (802) 442-5401, http://www.bennington.edu. A small liberal-arts college (600 students) where students help design their own programs. Strong in music and the arts.

College of the Atlantic, 105 Eden Street, Bar Harbor, ME, 04609, (800) 528-0025, inquiry@ecology.coa.edu, http://www.coa.edu. It's devoted to the study of ecology. Situated on a grand old estate on scenic Frenchman's Bay, it is within walking distance of the Atlantic Ocean and Acadia National Park. Students design their own programs within the areas of environmental design, environmental sciences, human studies, and public policy.

Colorado College, 14 East Cache La Poudre Street, Colorado Springs, CO, 80903, admissions@coloradocollege.edu, http://www.coloradocollege.edu. The academic year is divided into eight blocks of time, each lasting three and a half weeks. During each block of time, students concentrate on a single course. Students may design their own majors, and there are concentrations in such areas as African-American, Asian, Latin American, and Urban Studies.

Cornish College of the Arts, 710 East Roy Street, Seattle, WA, 98102, (800) 726-ARTS, admissions@cornish.edu, http://www.cornish.edu. Located in the heart of Seattle, Cornish Institute focuses on the arts—ceramics, sculpture, design, and dance. Students have to find their own housing, since the college isn't a residential one. Special attention is paid to students who are differently abled, especially those in wheelchairs: lowered telephones and specially equipped restrooms are a few of the accommodations available.

Earlham College, National Road West, Richmond, IN, 47374-4095, (800) 327-5426, http://www.earlham.edu. This college was established by the Society of Friends but is nonsectarian. Students are encouraged to design their own programs and take part in any one of the 27 programs offered in foreign countries. Virtually the entire campus is wheelchair accessible.

Embry-Riddle Aeronautical University, 600 South Clyde Morris Boulevard, Daytona Beach, FL, 32114-3900, (800) 862-2416, admit@db.erau.edu, http://www.embryriddle.edu. A unique university that is located at Daytona Beach Regional Airport. There is a second campus in Prescott, Arizona. Undergraduate degree programs are in aviation education, including pilot training.

Gallaudet University, 800 Florida Avenue, NE, Washington, DC, 20002-3695, admissions.office@gallaudet.edu, http://www.gallaudet.edu. This is the only private liberal-arts college for the deaf. Offers an intensive one-year precollege remedial program for students with academic deficiencies.

Goshen College, 1700 South Main Street, Goshen, IN, 46526, (800) 348-7422, admissions@goshen.edu, http://www.goshen.edu. Founded by the Mennonite Church, this college offers a study-service trimester abroad: 14 weeks of work and study. Requires international studies for graduation. Campus is wheelchair accessible and can provide sign language courses and interpreters for the hearing impaired.

Howard University, 2400 Sixth Street, NW, Washington, DC, 20059, (202) 806-6100, admission@howard.edu, http://www.howard.edu. This college's mission is to make higher education available to African-American students. Virtually the entire campus is wheelchair accessible. Counselors are available to help students with other special needs.

Landmark College, River Road South, Putney, VT, 05346, (802) 387-6718, http://www.landmark.edu. This is an extension of the Landmark School and is a four-year college specifically designed for students with learning disabilities.

Lincoln University, 1570 Baltimore Pike, P.O. Box 179, Lincoln University, PA, (610) 932-8300, http://www.lincoln.edu. One of the earliest black colleges, Lincoln counts Thurgood Marshall among its alumni. A recent expansion project has included over $29 million in improvements to the campus.

New College of the University of South Florida, 5700 North Tamiami Trail, Sarasota, FL, 34243-2197, (941) 359-4269, ncadmissions@sar.usf.edu, http://www.newcollege.usf.edu. The campus, which overlooks Sarasota Bay, is situated on the grounds of the former Ringling Brothers estate. The college has strong programs in the liberal arts, including environmental studies, English, fine and performing arts, philosophy, math, and sciences. Students receive written evaluations instead of grades. They are encouraged to design their own majors. All students are required to do independent studies.

Shimer College, P.O. Box 500, Waukegan, IL, 60079, (847) 623-8400, admissions@shimer.edu, http://www.shimer.edu. This college offers early admission to qualified students who have not completed high school. Core curriculum centers around the Great Books of the Western World, but students may create their own majors.

Texas A&M University at Galveston, P.O. Box 1675, Galveston, TX, 77553-1675, (877) 322-4443, seaaggie@tamug.tamu.edu, http://www.tamug.tamu.edu. This small liberal-arts and science college boasts that "the ocean is our classroom." Situated on beautiful Galveston Island, it overlooks the *Elissa,* a restored 1877 tall ship. TAMUG offers degrees in marine biology, marine fisheries, oceanography, maritime administration, and many other majors having to do with the sea. In addition, students can elect to sit for a Merchant Marine exam upon graduation and earn either a Third Mate's deck license or a Third Assistant Engineer's license. They may also train for the U.S. Coast Guard Reserve or U.S. Naval Reserve. Part of their training is done on the *Texas Clipper II*, a former U.S. Navy vessel. College freshmen can take their first college credits at sea.

World College West, 101 South San Antonio Road, Petaluma, CA, 94952. The average age of first-year students at World College West is 20 years. All first-year courses are team taught and interdisciplinary. Second-year students may study and work in either Nepal or Mexico. Third-year students may study in China. This experimental college places emphasis on academic study and cooperative governance. Study abroad—though optional—is encouraged. The academic year is divided into four 12-week quarters. Students study full time for two quarters and work in paying jobs for two.

Sometimes a two-year or community college will be just what you are looking for, especially for students who have stopped out for a while or those who need to upgrade their academic skills. Your own local community college may offer the opportunity to get back into the swing of academic life. Some offer intensive English as a Second or Other Language courses, others unique programs leading to an associate of arts or science degree that can't be obtained anywhere else. Three which I found particularly intriguing are:

Bel Rea Institute of Animal Technology, 1681 South Dayton, Denver, CO, 80231, (800) 950-8001, admissions@bel-rea.com, http://www.bel-rea.com. The Institute offers an associate degree in animal technology. Courses run for six consecutive quarters, including summers, for 18 months. Students attend classes for five quarters and take part in a paid internship program during the sixth quarter. The degree prepares them for paraprofessional work in veterinary medicine.

New England Culinary Institute, 250 Main Street, Montpelier, VT, 05602, (877) 223-6324, http://www.neculinary.com. What sets this two-year program apart from other culinary institutes is that it offers paid internships both in the United States and abroad.

Navajo Community College, Tsaile, AZ, 86556, and P.O. Box 580, Shiprock, New Mexico, 876420, louise@crystal.ncc. cc.nm.us, http://crystal.ncc.cc.nm.us. This is the first Native American–founded and –operated college in the United States. Begun in both Arizona and New Mexico in 1968, Navajo Community College offers numerous associate of arts degrees, including one in Navajo bilingual education.

A MONG THE MOST USED BOOKS IN ANY LIBRARY ARE THOSE THAT DESCRIBE COLLEGES AND UNIVERSITIES. You can always spot them because the covers quickly get battered through constant usage. Here are some that you may want to browse through. Most of these are revised frequently.

American Universities and Colleges, 16th ed. Washington: American Council on Education. Describes approximately 2,200 accredited institutions.

Chronicle Four-Year College Databook. Moravia, NY: Chronicle Guidance Publications. Summarizes information on approximately 2,200 four-year colleges.

College Blue Book, 31st ed. New York: Macmillan. A five-volume set that includes descriptions of colleges and universities and financial-aid offerings.

The College Board College Handbook, 4th ed. New York: The College Board. Summarizes information on 3,000 two- and four-year colleges.

The College Money Handbook, 21st ed. Princeton: Peterson's Guides. Cites costs at four-year colleges and provides background information on the financial-aid process.

Community, Junior and Technical College Directory. Washington: American Association of Community and Junior Colleges. Describes accredited two-year colleges.

Index of Majors and Graduate Degrees, 26th ed. New York: The College Board. Lists approximately 400 majors and tells which colleges offer them.

The Insider's Guide to the Colleges. New York: St. Martin's Press. Developed by the *Yale Daily News.* Presents the students' view of various colleges and universities.

Peterson's Competitive Colleges, 24th ed. Princeton: Peterson's Guides. Describes approximately 400 colleges with high admissions standards.

Peterson's Guide to Colleges with Programs for Students with Learning Disabilities or Attention Deficit Disorder. Princeton: Peterson's Guides. Describes colleges for special-needs students.

Peterson's Four-Year Colleges. Princeton: Peterson's Guides. Describes more than 2,100 accredited colleges and universities.

Peterson's Two-Year Colleges. Princeton: Peterson's Guides. Profiles more than 1,700 two-year colleges.

For Parents Only

THIS IS THE ONLY SECTION IN THE BOOK NOT DIRECTED TO STUDENTS. Instead, it is an open letter to your parents.

Dear Mom and Dad,

Being a conscientious parent of teenage kids today is probably almost as difficult as being a teenager. Our kids live in a world not of their making. More dangerous stuff is readily available to young people today than there ever was when we were their age. They are constantly faced with difficult choices we never had to consider: drugs, alcohol, lethal weapons, an increasingly polluted environment, a rapidly changing economy, and technology that is changing the way we study and work almost daily. Our concept of family life is also undergoing vast changes. Both we and our children often have to deal with painful situations that were completely unknown to older generations.

In addition to trying to cope with all the forces outside of themselves, today's youth are grappling with the same big questions we and our parents and grandparents dealt with: Who am I? What do I really believe in? Do I look all right? Am I attractive (or handsome) enough to attract that guy or gal sitting next to me? Do my parents love me? Am I in control of my life? Am I making the right choice? What's the purpose of my life? Will I be able to get a job when I'm through with school?

What may be the biggest surprise is that despite all of the stresses and the unknowns, our children have an incredible spirit of adventure. They are ready and willing to take some risks early in their lives because they sense that when they are older, those opportunities might not be available to them.

Perhaps the most difficult thing parents of teenagers have to cope with is their children's passion. Most 16- and 17-year-olds aren't often very adept at presenting a cogent and well-thought-out argument, especially to the people who mean the most—Mom and Dad. When kids discuss their plans with their friends, it all seems to make good sense. When the same kid tries to explain to a parent why he or she wants to work for a year or two, or study abroad, the words tend to tumble out in unintended abruptness. What begins as a discussion can quickly turn to anger and can end in a failure of understanding on both sides.

I guess we all have some sort of notion of what we'd like our children to do and be. We want them to move ahead with a good education, a secure future, and a lot of joy and happiness. There probably isn't a parent alive who doesn't want his or her child to avoid youthful mistakes. Yet we all know that no child grows up without making decisions that have turned out to be wrong, without arguing with parents, without striking out on his or her own. My writing teacher used to remind her class that without conflict, there is no story. And in real life, without conflict, a person doesn't change and grow.

Several parents whose children were interviewed for this book were kind enough to share their feelings about the paths their offspring had taken.

Robert Sigmon's daughter, Kiran, took time out between high school and college to join other young people on special projects in New Zealand and China. Kiran earned all of her travel money on her own. Mr. Sigmon, who is the associate director of an outreach education program at Wake Medical Center in Raleigh, North Carolina, is delighted with the challenges Kiran sought out, "although it is partly genetic," he says, not all together jokingly. "Her mother, whose parents were missionaries in China, and I actually met in Pakistan. What is especially gratifying is that Kiran accepted the responsibility for what she's doing. I think she'll land on her feet. . . . A lot of parents asked me how I could have let her go off like that—and my answer is I didn't let her go. She just went. All kids should have their own odyssey between the ages of 16 and 20."

"Well, Amity seemed to be getting bored with what high school was offering her," said her father, John Weiss. "It seemed to me that this [the United World College of the Adriatic] was just made for her. Since fifth grade she's been interested in international affairs, and she saw an opportunity to broaden her horizons there. At the same time, we were very impressed with the commitment of the school to offer service programs, and that seemed to blend in with her aspirations." Even though Amity had to sacrifice a year to go there, the rewards were worth it, her father said. "She was definitely tested as a person, in her flexibility socially and her intellectual agility and the strength of her convictions, which she knew would be tested. This, of course, is after the fact, when we saw how she had processed this experience. But of course we felt that we [parents] still had a lot to teach her, and she was going to be away for two years. You know, it's been great fun to be her father and to learn with her. But she had her wings, and she was ready to use them."

My plea to parents is to set aside your notions of what you want for your kids and really listen to what they are saying. Some of their ideas and goals may sound totally naive, even crazy. And you may be tempted to tell them so. Don't. Let them talk. Some of their hopes and dreams may break your heart in their simple yearning. Some of those desires may touch your own hidden dreams, and you may be astounded to find how much like you your children really are—or how much like a half-forgotten member of your family.

I interviewed dozens of young people for this book. Each was simply wonderful to talk with. They were full of plans and full of life. They were thrilled that I wanted to know what they'd done. They were honored that I wanted to know how they figured things out. Some of them confess that after talking to me, they decided to make some changes in their plans. Those young people who had stopped out for a year or two before going on to college had such a marvelous sense of purpose. One of my respondents had stayed out of school for four years—and I know that his parents were fearful that he'd never go to college. Yet, once he made up his mind, he went through a five-year undergraduate and M.B.A. program in three years. Today he is an accountant, married, and lives in Philadelphia.

All kids are not alike. They learn in different ways and at different rates. We all recognize this in little children—why should we expect our teens to be any different?

If your children complain about not learning anything in high school, listen to what they are saying. Maybe they've gotten all they can out of the place. They, better than anyone else, know what they are capable of. Give them a chance. If going to college early is what they really want to do, encourage them. Explore the options. Don't let young minds wither in an uninteresting and mind-deadening high school setting. On the other hand, take care not to push them into early college. And let your child know that if it doesn't work out, that's OK, too. There really are lots of options out there, and lots of things to try.

And what if your son or daughter has been a mediocre student, has been labeled "learning disabled," or has other disabilities? That child, who has not been successful in a traditional school for whatever reason, has innate gifts and abilities that need to be uncovered. What you can do as a parent is to show that you have enough faith in your kid to seek out a school that will help him or her reach the potential that is there. Don't give up on your child.

I believe the more you treat teenagers with trust and respect, the more they will take up the challenge to act in responsible ways. You may say, "Yeah, sure. But you don't know my kid." And that is perfectly true. But as a person who has spent a major part of her adult life teaching and writing about kids and education (and whose own three kids provided moments of high and low drama), I do know that the more you try to push young people into a mold, the more they will rebel. The sooner teenagers have the opportunity to make decisions for themselves, the sooner they will be in control of their own lives—and take responsibility for their successes and their failures.

The reward for encouraging your children to make their own choices and giving them enough help to allow them to be successful is that the trust and respect you offer gets returned—albeit later. Sometimes much later. Hang in there. It is worth it.

I hope this modest book will help your son or daughter make some important decisions about his or her future—and that you will find it within yourselves to support his or her choices.

Sincerely,
Bryna J. Fireside